Divya

The Rainbow Child

"It was a joy seeing the book come alive… every sequence is well-explained, brings out the external details and the inward developments as well. The story boldly raises certain delicate issues – 'mercy killing', 'conversion', etc. – and lucidly answers them without going into contradictions. Those who are endowed with spiritual tastes are led to appreciate that it is *Samvit* which sustains life, not stem cells."

Swami Ishwaranandagiri Maharaj
Sant Sarovar, Mount Abu

Dwaraknath Reddy is a spiritual seeker, his self-enquiry driven by Ramana Maharshi's initiative: "Who Am I?" An M.S. in chemical engineering from USA, he has written books on pure philosophy, but has also assessed the concept of Reality through the scientific frame of relativity. *Divya: The Rainbow Child* is his only foray into fiction so far. Written in his 85th year, this novel bears the potent message of philosophy coming to the rescue of ailing humanity. The author's considerable monetary wealth, earned by fostering a thriving industry for fifty years, has been formed into Ramanarpanam Trust to support and empower families living below the poverty line in city slums and rural or tribal tracts.

Divya
THE RAINBOW CHILD

DWARAKNATH REDDY

ZEN
PUBLICATIONS
A DIVISION OF MAOLI MEDIA PRIVATE LIMITED

First Zen Publications Edition: February 2015

PUBLISHED BY
ZEN PUBLICATIONS
A Division of Maoli Media Private Limited
60, Juhu Supreme Shopping Centre,
Gulmohar Cross Road No. 9, JVPD Scheme,
Juhu, Mumbai 400 049. India.
Tel: +91 9022208074
eMail: info@zenpublications.com
Website: www.zenpublications.com

Cover Illustrations by Lalithaa Thyagarajan

Cover & Book Design by Red Sky Designs, Mumbai

ISBN 978-93-84363-51-2

To Bhagavan Sri Ramana Maharshi

Who, at the age of sixteen, attained in himself the non-dual bliss of Enlightenment, and, at the age of seventy, allowed his mortal frame to be racked by the torturous cancer of carcinoma; whose body suffered immense pain, but who knew that he was not the body, for he was and is pure Consciousness – Sat-Chit-Ananda – beyond the changes of birth and death, beyond time.

Bhagavan, may we aspire to realize the Truth you manifested for our sake.

❦

Question: People speak of karma and retribution.

Maharaj: It is merely a gross approximation. In reality, we are all creators and creatures of each other, causing and bearing each other's burden.

Question: So the innocent suffers for the guilty?

Maharaj: In our ignorance, we are innocent; in our actions, we are guilty. We sin without knowing and suffer without understanding. Our only hope: to stop, to look, to understand and to get out of the traps of memory. For memory feeds imagination, and imagination generates desire and fear.

Nisargadatta Maharaj, *I Am THAT*

FOREWORD

BY DR. ANAND K. KHAKHAR

※

Dwaraknath Reddy's *Divya* is a story that could happen in any of our homes, but it is no less poignant for that. As a hepato-biliary and pancreatic surgeon with several years of hospital experience, I have seen this same heartbreaking sequence of events over and over again: A perfectly healthy child – or so it seems – suddenly falls victim to cancer and fades away before our very eyes. A pointless, tragic end – that is our first, instinctive, reactionary view, but though I may not seem qualified to judge the spiritual content of this book, the author expresses a clear view that there is nothing in the universe that is meaningless and purposeless; every life (and every death) is firmly woven into the cosmic tapestry. This book provides a glowing picture of spiritual evolution that more than compensates for the physical degeneration of its protagonist.

The author deserves our kudos for thoroughly researching and accurately reproducing all the details of a typical case of cancer and the medical treatment given in response, in all their escalating stages. And he has gone further, sensitively exploring the psychological effects on the patient and immediate family members and friends as well. All in all, this is a book to be as slowly savoured as an elixir promising eternal life.

Dr. Anand K. Khakhar is the Program Director and Senior Consultant, Liver Transplant and Hepato-biliary Surgery, at the Center for Liver Disease and Transplantation, Apollo Hospitals, Chennai.

FOREWORD

by YOGACHARYA C. SASHIDHAR REDDY

✿

The state of equanimity is a balance of the 'head' and the 'heart', an indicator of a divine instrument who is on the last rungs of perfection. Such a ripened soul exudes the fragrance of divinity and soothes the suffering souls around. It also lights lamps within, removing darkness (ignorance), and strengthening by steadfastly showing the true path.

It is indeed a joy going through this gem of a book, which fills us with the fragrance emitting from the beautiful, equanimous soul of Dwaraknath Reddy. This is indeed a much-needed, practical book which lifts our minds from the terrestrial plane to our consciousness (God), where true solace and strength is found. This novel can be a crucial aid for the questioning, and often depressed, patients coping with cancer or other critical, life-threatening health problems. It can help them reach out to their higher consciousness for the courage to overcome their fears of debility and death, bringing them closer to their Self, the Creator. It is a special book, in tune with our times, meeting the need of the hour.

Yogacharya C. Sashidhar Reddy is a senior and close disciple of Grand Master Choa Kok Sui, founder of the International Pranic Healing Movement and Arhatic Yoga (established in more than 80 countries, with his books and meditation tapes being available in 30 languages). He is the President and Managing Trustee of the GMCKS Yoga Vidya Pranic Healing Foundation Trust, India. Yogacharya Sasidhar is an international yoga teacher and the founder of SOHAM (School of Higher Awareness and Meditation) at Hyderabad.

INTRODUCTION

❦

Sorrow and sickness haunt the lives of the rich and the poor alike today. Society has lost its age-old tradition of surrender to the higher Cosmic Order which governs the universe and bestows both peace and prosperity on the human mind. Feeling forlorn and forsaken, helpless and haunted, we cannot face approaching death when the time comes.

What happens to a middle-class family when confronted by major health problems – cancer, kidney transplant, heart surgery, liver failure, cerebral haemorrhage, paralysis and many others? Medical science has treatments within limitations, but the cost and suffering and uncertainty always sink the family that is trying to save a soul.

Man's mind must abide in the knowledge of the Cosmic Order, the laws of life as ordained in Creation. It is within the reach of each one of us. Only then can we face ordeals serenely. Mankind can bear 'the slings and arrows of outrageous fortune' only through such an understanding of cosmic purpose and method.

Divya's story is of a life that could transcend death through right knowledge. The purpose of writing about Divya is only to show despairing humanity the direction to achieve renewed strength and redemption.

Dwaraknath Reddy
August 2012

1

Divya was fifteen when the dark, menacing clouds came over the horizon of her life. When the storm of adversity begins to brew amidst the blinding whiplashes and deafening thunder of impending disaster, who can predict if the fury of the floods will sweep away home and hearth, or if a relenting Providence will mitigate their ferocity and permit survival? Who can know the future?

Everyone in their colony remembered Divya as a young girl. She had been so irresistible that all the other parents ungrudgingly paid the tribute of calling her the sweetest child in the neighbourhood. Some even dubbed her "our little rainbow" affectionately.

When Divya was ten, her teacher taught the class about sunlight being a composite of seven colours. She explained how sunrays, refracted and dispersed through drops of water or mist, are split into seven colours to form the colourful arch adorning the heavens. The little girl sensed the secret of this delight of Nature, and danced down the road on her way home that evening, singing:

I am born of a raindrop
To sing, to dance, and to hop.

A rainbow did seem to enter the house in her wake.

Divya's home was located in what had originally been a rural area, but was now one of the outermost suburbs of the expanding metropolis of Chennai.

Her father, Govinda, had been a diligent student in his day and had managed to, against all odds, obtain a degree in mechanics, secure a job in an engineering firm, and rise to the position of a departmental manager in its factory. He was an honest, hard-working man, aware of his official duties and his family responsibilities. His ambition was to be promoted, through his merit and performance, to the post of factory manager.

His wife, Geeta, a pleasant and energetic young woman, was a good wife and a good mother. Their firstborn, Niranjan, was two years older than Divya. Geeta was diligent in her housework, keeping their two-bedroom home meticulously clean, and doing all the cooking and shopping for provisions by herself. Their part-time maid came in daily to sweep the floors, clean the dishes and wash the clothes. With two children in school, and their college education to provide for eventually, the need to practise frugal thrift and save for the future dominated the lives of Govinda and Geeta.

Considering her rural, almost rustic background, Geeta had done remarkably well in even completing high school, but the demands of a communal life left her with no freedom to study further. She stayed at home, learnt domestic skills, and looked after her parents who were bent low before their time with problems pecuniary and physical, till relenting fate brought her a good alliance and she was married to Govinda. She now had a better home and status, but the family had to set the goals higher, strive harder and raise the whole standard of living for the next generation. Geeta worked on enhancing her knowledge through her children's textbooks to help them in their studies. In this, her husband shared as much as he could, given the pressures of his own work. It was a well-knit, harmonious and fairly disciplined family, grateful for blessings received and willing to work hard for its own betterment.

This serenity in the family, this peace in spite of strife and struggle for material adequacy, had its basis in its eldest member, Raman, Govinda's aging father. Raman had lost his wife to typhoid several years earlier. In those communities, at sixty, one was already living on borrowed time, with the poorly nourished and overworked bodies worn out and falling apart. That she could hold the infant Divya in her arms for a while was itself a fulfilment which had made the grandmother's farewell easier.

Since then, Raman had lived with Govinda and Geeta. He was respectfully and affectionately accommodated in their home. His meagre pension as a retired headmaster of a high school was in some measure a contribution to the family budget.

He sometimes visited, by turns, his other sons, Ravi and Sekhar, who lived elsewhere in Chennai and held managerial jobs, earning salaries that provided a fairly decent living to their families. He stayed for about a week at a time with them, once or twice a year, and otherwise lived quietly with Govinda's family.

He had been a dedicated teacher always, keen to communicate and comfort, concerned about the future of the youngsters he taught. He considered it his duty to inculcate the joy of learning in the rather unruly and indifferent kids of poor, illiterate farm labourers and construction workers. His aim was that school should be for them not an infliction reluctantly suffered, but a benediction gladly awaited.

With love and laughter, always caring and sharing, the patient, pleasant teacher had nurtured generations out of which had emerged scholars, with their standard of life elevated several-fold. Some had even gone on to become doctors, lawyers, engineers and, Raman recollected with a bemused smile, lecturers in colleges. He felt blessed. Teaching was a sacred profession.

From an early age, Raman had been spiritual by nature, easily and instinctively feeling the presence of a supreme Order and Authority in his life, no less than in the whole of creation. Therefore he looked for and took advantage of every opportunity to get instructed in religious and philosophical teachings. He would pedal his cycle for miles willingly if any discourse or chanting programme was held within reach. These talks were often couched in basic expositions, intended for an audience with no scholarship or sharpened intellect, but, to one who could sieve and shift the husk from the grain, great truths were revealed in those simple terms.

Raman's mind and heart worked in great affinity, and often tears, rising unbidden, comforted him with the conviction that a personal truth of one's own being could reach out to God and be graciously received. He read whatever books he could borrow from libraries, and structured for himself a knowledge base that contained concepts of creator and creation in credible, and even irrefutable, terms.

The mighty declarations of Vedantic lore opened their mystic secrets to his searching mind. The assumption of a personalized identity for the human individual was itself the fundamental error. It then followed that all subsequent conclusions were in error, being founded on a primordial ignorance of the Truth. That Truth is what is called God.

No man is an island. 'Do not send to know for whom the bell tolls, for it always tolls for thee.' The reality of oneself is that one is Total Consciousness, not a fragmented, and thereby limited, individual; not a mere flash in time between the womb and the tomb. Seen thus, the seeker of truth becomes one with the mind's concept of God. Thence follow the ultimate scriptural declarations: *Ahaṃ Brahmāsmi* (I am Brahman) and *Tat tvam asi* (That thou art).

As these illuminating thoughts took possession of him, they became the very substratum of his existence. The purpose, direction, and fulfilment of his life lay in so living within the mind that this objective knowledge could become subjective experience.

This heightened goal and dedication made him a rare human being indeed, one with pristine values and an understanding of universal harmony, a man of enduring peace. He was much more than a teacher of a curriculum; he was a teacher of life.

With his perception of the divine dispensation that ran unerringly through all lives and all events, and with a peaceful acceptance of destiny's writ, he saw how the threads of personal lives were interwoven in the matrix of the cosmic fabric, so that the totality, when seen truly, was only a single movement in time and space, with no inherent discord.

Yet, individual minds, unable to see this grandeur in the Creator's scheme, laid out their own demands and courted grief and resentment and suffering when their desires were not fulfilled. They had not a clue to the basic tenet that there has to be a causal rightness to the demands one may make, in terms of the progression of one's own life.

In the causal continuity that relates action and reaction, there must be a deserving to justify a demanding. One who approaches the unfolding phenomena of life with this fundamental rightness of intellect is naturally calm, secure, and peaceful at all times. That alone is a life lived to its true potential.

2

To Raman today, memory brought back Divya as a twelve-year-old girl. "Ramana *Thatha*, Ramana *Thatha!*" had rung the childish voice in crisp tones, as the mellow light of early evening fell upon the lazy street. It was quite usual for Divya, returning from her day at school, to shout thus to her grandfather,[1] and she expected him to step out on to the porch and respond to her call. So he called back warmly, "Yes, Divya, come."

And she replied, "Thatha, look at me. Can you see me?" Bending her hands sideways in front of her and lifting the palms to form an arch with fingers interlocked beneath her chin, she jumped in a jig from side to side and then ran forward, singing:

> Here I come, the rainbow band,
>
> Lightly arching over the land,
>
> I am robed in colours seven,
>
> I have come to earth from heaven.

---

1 *The children always called Raman 'Ramana Thatha', in a sing-song manner.*

She turned towards the doorway of her house, and beaming with the joy of sheer living, hugged her grandfather, then ran in to hold her mother. A snack and a glass of milk were hers to take. Daddy would return from work much later, while her brother would linger a while longer on the school playfield. She had a quick wash and came back to Thatha, who was lighting the lamp at the niche reserved as the place of worship in their home. It was their routine that a brief pooja was offered at this hour of approaching dusk.

Thatha would tell Divya, in a low voice, that when the sun had not yet set and the darkness of night had not quite arrived, when the twin aspects of creation – be they day and night, knowledge and ignorance, or joy and sorrow – seemed to merge, lighting the prayer lamp symbolised lighting the lamp of one's mind in this homage to God, the Creator, who alone was everything always, the unchanging Truth amidst all changes.

Divya would close her eyes softly and nod her head in approval, for she sensed, in her own simple way, the meaning of Thatha's words and accepted their validity.

And Thatha's intention was only this: that little Divya should have an instinctive grasp of the presence, power, and rightness of a supreme God. Let her question all of it in the years ahead, let her doubt, argue, deny and debate, but, for now, let her love and accept it instinctively the way only a child's innocence can.

The mellowed fruit of Ramana Thatha's wisdom and the budding instincts of little Divya shared a common root.

One day, Divya came home from school as usual, but her chirping gaiety was absent, and she called out to Thatha in a melancholy tone. Sensing the shift in her mood, he waited for her to come close. "What is the matter, Divya?" he asked.

"Thatha, you know Sharada, my friend and classmate? Her

father dropped her at the school gate morning as usual and went away. There were hardly any other children outside, only I happened to be there. Thatha, Sharada just stood there, with her back to the gate, and across the empty road she saw a cute puppy, looking at her and vigorously wagging its tail as if wanting to meet her. Sharada impulsively darted across the street.

"A motorcycle was going down the lonely road and though the rider swerved, he hit Sharada. She fell down, writhing in pain and crying. I shouted for help, and our teacher, who was nearby, rushed out and arranged for Sharada to be carried in. The teacher rang up Sharada's mother, then got a car to take Sharada to the hospital. We learnt later that she had fractured her leg and had cuts on her hands. I saw blood on her clothes, Thatha. Thatha, will Sharada die?" And Divya burst into tears.

"Surely she will not die, Divya. The fracture will heal, though it may take time. Maybe a month. She will then come back to school and play with you."

"I want that, Thatha. We always play 'catch-me' and I run so fast that even God can't catch me!"

"God can, Divya, because He is everywhere already."

"True, you told me that before. Then, Thatha, why doesn't God catch me?"

"Because He too is playing the game. He wants to see where you will catch Him."

"Oh, it is like that! He is there, but I don't see Him, and so I don't catch Him, and He is laughing silently … Thatha?"

"Yes, Divya."

"Was it the puppy's fault that Sharada was hurt?"

"I would not say so. The puppy naturally showed its love."

"I think so too, Thatha. Later I went up to the pup. It looked into my eyes so sadly. I think there were tears in its eyes. Thatha, do puppies cry as I cry?"

"They do, Divya, and for the same reasons. They have feelings the same way you have. All things in Nature suffer hurt and sadness, hunger and betrayal. Love is wherever life is."

Then wanting to pull Divya out of her sorrow, Ramana Thatha said; "Have your milk and wash up and come for pooja." When Divya did so, Thatha said, "You light the lamp, remembering God and Sharada."

Divya lit the lamp. "Thatha, shall I pray to God that Sharada may have no pain?"

"You may pray so, child, and maybe, reaching Sharada, your prayer will quieten her mind. But remember that nature has to run its course. Pain too is a part of God's law at work and has a role to play. Wouldn't you rather pray that Sharada should accept that what has happened to her, while appearing to hurt her needlessly, is actually God's will for her, with His love and care for her inherent in it? Let her understand God and not accuse Him."

"Yes, Thatha, if God is not pure love, He is not God. If He is pure love, He does only what is best for us."

The simple prayer ended, but Divya could not leave the train of thought. "Yet, Thatha, such a conclusion is difficult to accept. Someone must be at fault for Sharada's injury. It wasn't the puppy. Was it the rider of the bike? The road was empty and Sharada was standing to one side, and then she ran across suddenly, so it wasn't the rider's fault. Could it be the fault of her daddy that he did not walk with her into the school? As usual, he left her safely at the gate and he had to go to his office on time. Was it Sharada's fault? Not unless it is a fault to feel love for a cuddly puppy. Then where lies the fault, Thatha?"

"Must there be a fault somewhere, Divya? Can it not be

that everything was right in its own way, being natural to that moment? What took place was an event, being the outcome of several natural contributory events. We call some events as accidents, as they are unusual and unexpected. Also, they are against our natural desires and result in pain, exertion, expense and anxiety. There is a cosmic rightness in everything that happens; otherwise we are saying that God does what should not be done, by intention or by mistake. It means God is the One who is at fault when what we call an accident happens."

"I think I can see what you mean, Thatha. God cannot be guilty of a fault in His action."

A moment of silent communication was ended by Niranjan bursting upon the scene with his brusque "Hi Thatha, hi Mom, hey Divya, you are not well or what?"

And Mummy, who had briefly learnt about Sharada, said, "Her friend had an accident. We will tell you later. How was your day?"

"I came first in the class in the midterm exams. Also, mom, my basketball coach praised my play. You should have seen my rival who is two inches taller; he looked two inches shorter then! He is such a proud guy."

"Watch out that you don't become a proud guy yourself," said Divya, laughing as she ducked and ran into the house.

"Wise dame," shouted her brother after her.

Laughter. Twelve-year-old sister. Fourteen-year-old brother. Stars in heaven waiting to be plucked by those whose minds could rise on tiptoe to reach upwards.

Yes, if so it was willed. But tomorrow is always hidden under today's sunset.

❧

3

It had become the normal practice that the three sons of Raman, the patriarch, gathered at one of the three homes with their families once every month or six weeks and had lunch together. Their affection and reverence for Raman was evident and the dignified elder showed his response in quiet serenity. It was the day to exchange news and views, as also to share concerns, prospects and plans, both individually and as a family.

The children loved to get together for fun and frolic, and there was more talking than listening! The ladies kept their council, preparing a sumptuous feast while discussing the restraints enforced on family budgets by the mounting prices of all foodstuffs, from milk to lentils to bananas, not to ignore the dues to housemaids, dhobis or plumbers, and what about transportation costs?

On this Sunday, the get-together was at Govinda's house. Only a month earlier, the city corporation had confirmed plans to lay an express circular road skirting the suburbs along a part of the city limits, so that it could link as a bypass with a six-lane highway that was almost completed, thus permitting fast and open access from the highway to the downtown metropolis and avoiding the over-congested traffic on the old city roads.

As fortune would have it, the three brothers had utilized their savings to buy some land, each in the suburban area that seemed most relevant to his needs, budget limitations, and reach of his workplace. Now the newly proposed ring road would be running close to their properties. They could hardly believe their luck. The value of their land had jumped threefold in one spurt, and surely looked set to double all over again. For their means, it was indeed a sudden inheritance.

"In divine dispensation, God gives and God takes. There is rightness to everything. We are entitled to feel happy when we are given, if we have the understanding not to feel deprived when it is taken. Such equanimity gives us the strength to live always with inner peace, because we are then in harmony with the cosmic law." Thus spoke Ramana Thatha in a quiet voice and his three sons heard him and let it pass, as is our wont with good advice.

Divya, who was, of all the children, the closest to Thatha, heard it too, and it sounded so true, so natural, that a lamp was lit in her heart.

Thus the sublime moment passed, half noticed, and an animated conversation took over, reviewing the economic conditions in the country and the rest of the world, the government's responses and restrictions, and how the future appeared for families like theirs. The children would have to pursue higher studies, medicine, engineering, law and IT being the preferred options, but any one of them would cost a fortune unless major scholarships were earned. The fathers would have to be diligent at work and qualify for rapid promotions, the mothers would have to be frugal – but how much could they save anyhow? – and, above all, the students should be motivated, guided, goaded, and relentlessly driven on the path of ambition. This was the discussion.

Only the elderly Raman listened, without dissent, without much comment, for he knew that the adult minds, already set in their fixed grooves, were not so pliable. Only Divya's was, even amongst the tender minds.

After the feast, which the kids ate with gusto, and the men with appreciation and relish (commenting in good humour that, this time, too many cooks did not spoil the broth, because each cook had wisely adopted one dish exclusively!), there was brief repose. Then the youngsters were free to play in the open spaces with a football and a couple of hula hoops, while the others gathered in a family circle around Raman.

Speaking gently and softly, Govinda, the eldest son, made easy conversation. "Father," he said, "with your blessings and our obedience to your sacred words, we, your three sons, have prospered and are placed comfortably enough. Our tribute to Mother and you has been that we have worked hard, remained steady, and lived without being corrupted by the distorted values of society. We will continue to live the same way, and we are grateful that we have your guidance. We are also fortunate in our partners – they all feel Mother's blessings instructing and aiding them."

Silence prevailed for a minute, a token of peaceful consent to what had been spoken. Raman said, "So it must have been. And so let it be. The will is His, while it must seem to be ours; the action is His, while ours are the hands that perform. The fruits are dispensed as ordained by Him, and causal correctness ensures that each gets his deserts exactly as deserved, never more and never less.

"The law of God is as beautiful as it is awesome. The past projects the present, and the present shapes the future, which gets recycled into the past. The flow and flux are continuous; it is one seamless, eternal movement. What you look upon as your individual destinies are, in truth, interwoven threads in cosmic destiny, but because of the separative assertion of individuality, one experiences, and surrenders to, a personalized destiny. So be it.

"But be consistent and accept personal responsibility for your being what you are, and for all that happens to you. As you think, so you act; as you act, so you become. This is the causal sequence; this alone is the method of fate, karma, destiny, causation – so many words, but one truth alone."

"But we are unable to see the links with any remembered past when the unexpected or the disastrous hits us with tyrannical ferocity," said one of his sons.

His brother endorsed the objection and expanded it. He said, "Crime and punishment must be related as cause and effect, and the connection must be perceivable. Otherwise, they would seem to be random and arbitrary, with no law or order in the flow of life's sequences, and no sustained justice in divine dispensation."

"Remember," said their father, "that the law is cosmic, whereas your perception of its workings, and your grasp of the interactions between those workings, are limited to the personal. The present flows from the past. The past is like a pack of cards which is shuffled by the hand of time as operated by causal determinism. You do not know which card will be turned up next from the deck, as you will see it only after it has been turned face up. Till then, it rests unknown. When it is dealt to you, you play it. You don't ask why that card turned up for you just then, for to fret or to ask that question is not in the spirit of the game.

"What you are referring to as punishments or rewards are certainly your true deserts, though the time sequence of action and reaction, virtue and reward, crime and punishment, cause and consequence, is not on any temporal scale that you can automatically determine or decipher. There is never the slightest distortion of the benign law."

There they let the matter rest for the day, to take it home for deep contemplation. Farewells were said lingeringly, and the two aged, small cars, always carefully tended, collected their respective families and gently set into motion. Divya and Niranjan were still waving their hands when no one could see them doing that any more.

4

Two days later, Divya was in a pensive mood, but that was nothing strange. She was a brilliant girl, a student of outstanding merit, first in her class and winner of many inter-school contests, lively and friendly. But she was by nature often contemplative and aloof, her thoughts mature beyond her years, her concerns transcending the mundane and touching ultimate meanings and purposes that few adults, caught in their material whirlpools, had even an inkling about. Ramana Thatha was the one with whom she could freely share those elated moods and compelling needs.

"Thatha," she said one evening, "at the family get-together that day, I was playing with my cousins, but my mind was elsewhere, seeking answers to the workings of fate, so I could not help overhearing quite a bit of what my uncles and Daddy and you were discussing. I could not quite understand all that was being said, Thatha, but the sense of it seemed to be that the causes for gladness or sadness are not often self-revealing. When my teacher rebukes me (which she hardly does!), I can understand my lapse. When my brother shares his only chocolate with me, the feeling of love is clear.

"But when my friend Sharada was hit by the stranger's motorbike, the link seemed missing, though there must be a causal link. There must be such a link, Thatha, I see that, otherwise justice would be reduced to mere chance, but I do not see that link. So I have to accept an unseen link. Is this faith? But in my physics and mathematics lessons, faith is not called for, is it? I work with facts that are real. I understand and accept them then and there. It is simple, clear, rational."

"You little eavesdropper!" said Thatha, in mock disapproval. "You have heard it all."

Divya giggled merrily. Then she continued with renewed earnestness: "Thatha, I heard also what you said in reply. You talked about a pack of cards being shuffled and the cards being dealt out. Whose is the hand that shuffles the pack, Thatha? It cannot be that of one of the players. My friends and I sometimes pass time playing cards. After shuffling, any card may be dealt, it depends on chance. Were you saying that God's hand shuffles the pack, and the cards of joy or sorrow are dealt out to us? If so, where is chance eliminated and rightness brought in? What is God's nature that He can know everything and manage everything accurately?"

Thatha knew he must now lay the foundations for Divya to, over a period of time, gain the right perception of what human wisdom at its pinnacle of understanding signifies by the word 'God'. So he spoke slowly, in measured tones, choosing his words with care. Perhaps the truth that has baffled many an adult seeker could reveal itself in the mind of this little girl because her mind was so uncluttered, so transparent, so genuine.

"Dear child," Thatha said, "you have asked what God's nature is. The truth is that God has no 'nature', yet all that is 'nature' to our mind is in Him or of Him. We humans have a 'nature' and that is formed by the texture of our individual minds. God is Consciousness. Grasp that, Divya, and the right understanding will follow. Listen carefully; I said, 'God is Consciousness'. I did not say 'God is conscious'. You and I are conscious. We are conscious of things. Those things may be other persons, or what is heard or remembered – objects, memories or desires. All these become thoughts at the mental plane. Mind is nothing but a flow of thoughts, and to think is to be conscious of a thing. In other words, Divya, I am saying that to be conscious is human, and to be Consciousness is divine. If a mind is a limited sphere of the capacity to be conscious, then the totality of the conscious activity of all minds in creation would be the Total Mind or Total Consciousness.

"It is in this dimension that you should conceive God. Then you will agree that anything and everything that is thought of in any mind is the content of consciousness, and is therefore 'known' to God. It is not a process of knowing as with you and me. As you breathe effortlessly, so God knows effortlessly. As a breath is not missed in you, a thought is not missed in him. God's operational system is a cosmic computer into which every thought of every mind is automatically and instantaneously fed and indelibly recorded. All the numerous factors that are linked to any event in this vast world of continuous action, interaction, and reaction are correlated by the cosmic computer and the output is accurate. Error is impossible.

"From this stems divine justice. The Intelligence that determines the sequence and consequence of these events may be thought of as the hand that shuffles all the facts that are fed into the cosmic computer and extracts the results that should follow in the determinism of cause-effect order. The temporal order is causal correctness. Such is the cosmic law and it flows on.

"I have tired you, my child. Let shades of this knowledge remain, that will do. We will have to return to it again and again."

"Fine, Thatha. I get a faint feel of it. God's ways are fascinating. Recently, our maths teacher indicated to us that a fascinating concept would be taught to us over the next two years, so beautiful that he termed it the romance of numbers. But even what my teacher called 'differential calculus' may be easier to understand than what you expound."

"It would be. God is the author of non-differential calculus."

"What was that? Say it again, Thatha."

"Never mind, child. Just an old man's prattle."

※

5

Niranjan was not less than an affectionate brother to Divya, but between a boy of fifteen and a girl of thirteen, the age gap seems not two but ten. So, on return from school, it would be a "Hi, girlie" and a pat on the cheek for Divya before he had to open up importantly on the trivia of the day before Thatha and Mummy – if Mummy had the patience – and of course it would be mostly about himself. Today they had a one-hour-a-side cricket match on the school grounds, and he was the opening fast bowler. In his third over, he was, on his own evidence, so fast that the batsman could hardly sight the ball. Surely – "God's truth, Thatha" – he had the captain of the opposing team plumb LBW – "Leg-before-wicket, Thatha" – but, the cheats, Thatha, the boy standing in as umpire was the best friend of that captain, and he said "Not out". "I told him he was blind."

"Better if you are not the appellant and the judge at the same time, Niranjan," said Thatha. "It is proper to respect the verdict of the referee, even when it is against you. It may be his honest conviction."

"Thatha, you don't know cricket," said Niranjan, comfortably superior. "Amma, what is there to eat this minute?

"Your thumb," shouted Divya from somewhere and hid herself.

That night, they talked about Niranjan's education. "I am studying for all I am worth," he said. "I do not miss a class. I even go to the library and study advanced texts. I want to be an engineer, Amma. My friends and their parents, some in very senior positions, always maintain that a prestigious MBA should go with a Master's in Engineering or Technology. Amma, I score around 80%, as you all know. I will try my hardest to go higher, but I cannot see myself exceeding 90%. Even that will not fetch me a scholarship. I want to succeed; once in a good job, I will climb to the top because, besides studies, I have strengths in other assets. (I am irresistible, he said to himself.) Thatha, Mom, what will it cost us for me to complete engineering and management degrees?"

"More than what we have, son," said Geetha with a sad smile. "We have to lower our sights."

"Mom, if I can get an engineering job, I can probably pay my way through MBA from my own earnings, can't I?"

"By then, we will already be much in debt," said Mom, pensively. There was a long moment's pause. "Entrance to technical courses costs a fortune. We are saving, but thousands are not lakhs." Another moment of silence. "Divya's marriage will also be a priority in a few years. She seems to be on course to academic excellence. If she unfortunately misses out on a scholarship to IIT… Enough for now. I have work in the kitchen." And she hid her tears.

Thatha, who had remained mostly silent till now, said, "Niranjan, I appreciate your concern. We must, of course, do the best that our efforts can achieve. Beyond that, we have to accept what providence decrees. The gardener tends to the whole orchard, but it may be that one tree bears luscious fruit while another remains barren. There are a myriad of factors that determine the outcome of each event. To know this is to have strength and equanimity – the strength to strive the hardest, the equanimity to accept peacefully whatever be the result."

"Thatha, you often talk to us of providence, God, causal rightness, and of our acceptance. Is that not a defeatist attitude, a weakness of personality?"

"Niranjan, for any happening, any event, change, or movement, there must be a cause. Whatever happens is caused to happen. Cause manifests as effect. Obviously, without a cause there can be no effect. Also, the effect then becomes the cause for the succeeding effect in the flow of time's sequence. To the enquiring mind, naturally, the question arises, 'What was the "first cause"? How did it appear without a prior cause?' That is where a concept of Providence or God has to be accommodated. 'God' is another term for 'Uncaused Cause'.

"You will say that this phrase is a contradiction in terms and therefore inadmissible. You will be right too, but only within your terms of verbal usage. Your language is within the framework of relativity, but we are shifting our reference to the Absolute. You are not alone in facing this paradox. The greatest physicists of the past hundred years have yet to answer in their scientific jargon the question of what triggered the explosion of a black hole into the Big Bang. The words they have, namely, gravity, electromagnetic radiation, or subatomic forces, do not meet the bill. They are talking of a Unified Field, but those again are empty words as yet.

"So, Niranjan, do not dismiss what the sages have said, but do continue to question them till you have transcended to a much higher understanding. You will get the answers only when knowledge transcends itself to become experience. Until then, think of the rationale of the causal connectivity that flows from the past into the future, determining and defining the present activity. Now go and play cricket."

Niranjan saw that this was beyond his capacity to see. Some reluctant respect was taking hold of him, making him uncomfortable. But he had the luxury of flippant bravado, especially with his indulgent grandfather. So he laughed vacantly and said, "Let me talk to my physics teacher." He stood up, and hugged his grandfather. "Thatha, God may be Bradman, but I will bowl him out as others have bowled Bradman before." And he disappeared.

Thatha let it rest there. Niranjan was not Divya. Niranjan would have to fight his personal battles for worldly prosperity and fame and handle success and failure as men of the world do, elated and dejected by turns, with never an end to the cascade of desires and demands; whereas Divya seemed to be lifted upon wings of intuition into spaces far higher than her intellect, exalted as that was in itself. She could sense a reality beyond the relative, a godhead behind the person, an eternity across the time-bound. Thatha wanted to bring this into sharper focus and make the Truth functional in her life, even at this tender age. He had the right words if she had the right will. And he was convinced she had.

6

Upon the far horizon, a small dark cloud arises, hiding an immense fury, and awaits its ordained time. In the heart of the mighty expanse we call the sky, a small column of spiralling wind shakes its mane impatiently, yet causes no stampede till its reins are slackened. Upon the limitless bosom of stretching waters, a wave arises to imply the seething might that will spread far, till the sea is a cauldron of wrath. Amidst the dense forest where no human foot has trod, where tooth, trunk, and horn rule the territory, a fire rises from the friction of wind-tossed bamboo groves, and smoulders till it will erupt in blazing flames that leap from treetop to treetop, leaving behind desolate ashes of destruction.

And then – but only then – the clouds disappear, the sun shines, the winds turn gentle, the forests sprout again, and it is as though it had never been any different, as though the fiends had never left their lairs. What wonder is there in this? If a seed thought of creation in the *sankalpa* of *Īśvara* could manifest the cosmic universes, what is not possible when His mind plays with the elements which are His toys?

Yet Raman knew that neither caprice nor carelessness has ever flawed the justice of a single event that has marked a footprint upon our earth, seemingly soon washed away, but, in truth, indelibly engraved upon the wrinkled face of Time. The event will hold its causal potential till the shuffling hand of causal justice turns it face upwards and brings about the related and righteous results at the appropriate moment. The cosmic management never blinks an eyelid and never permits an error.

Time is unlimited, whereas our bodies are limited in time. The mind has its continuity in time till it merges in its source, which is unbroken, undisturbed Consciousness. But bodies have no kinship to eternity, as we all know too well, having witnessed birth, disease, and death. Bodies are mechanical devices in the cosmic scheme, equipments that manifest the personal energy of a conscious mind.

Equipments eventually wear out and break down, or are broken before their time by impacts they cannot withstand. An electric bulb burns out with prolonged use, or the filament may break due to a severe jolt, or it may fuse due to a high voltage surge. Whatever the reason, the bulb will 'die' one day, but the electrical energy that gave 'life' to the bulb by manifesting as light in it, that energy does not perish with the bulb. It lives on and manifests again in some other equipment.

What happens to our bodies is secondary, Raman reflected – what is important is the state of the mind and its causal continuity. The mind will continue its compulsive passage through time until we understand the inherent error in our concept of 'reality', which is nothing but relativity. It is only then that we can regain unity with the Absolute, which is our own true nature.

The seeming riddle of accidents, unexpected calamities, and 'untimely' death can be solved by understanding this vital truth. The psyche which inhabits the human body is a bird of passage upon a misguided voyage. It tries to actualize its instinct for eternal, abiding happiness and peace through relationships and acquisitions.

Living thus, our timeless psyche transmigrates through body after body with limited lifespan. What we call life and death are not the beginnings and ends we mistake them to be, but only milestones on a winding road. The broken or 'fused' body is discarded, but the soul endures in an altered plane of consciousness, and, in the ripeness of time, gets re-slotted into a different body.

Raman had heard gurus use a familiar experience as an example: when we dream, what happens seems real, even though our body is reclining in sleep and does not contribute to the perceived actions and feelings. Our physical frame can thus be 'dead' to the experience through which our mind 'lives'.

Mercifully, the redemption from bondage is also built into this cycle of birth and death, so that no one is condemned to bear forever the cross of unfulfilled desire and unrequited love. These are only the erroneous compulsions of a misguided mentality. The remedy lies in right knowledge acquired through self-enquiry; or, if one is predisposed by an intuitive revelation and an instinctive acceptance to see the face of Divinity behind all existence, let one surrender to Its benign supremacy heart and soul.

Either way, through enquiry or surrender, the fetters that bind the mind are broken, and in an indescribable, new dimension, freedom and peace are instantly possessed.

A fledgling possibility of such freedom and peace was what Ramana Thatha saw in Divya, and he nurtured that budding potential at every opportunity. But right now, the small dark cloud of unknown portent came upon Divya in the form of a fever.

7

Two more months had passed by. Divya was always the toast of her class and beyond. She was noticed and admired in inter-school circles, and was a crown jewel in the cherished reputation of her school. Yet, due to the mellowness of her nature, she was always lovable and humble, gentle and cheerful. She had no arrogance and no halo round her head, only a happy glow in her eyes and a smile on her lips that spoke of loving and being loved. What a child!

One day, she returned home from school an hour earlier than usual. She had fever and a running nose and said she felt fatigued. The sickness had come upon her suddenly and she could not just shake it off. She managed to haltingly eat a slice of toast and drink a glass of milk. Then she slept. She seemed to have flu-like symptoms, not uncommon in the season.

She should be better with rest for a day or two, her family thought, and tried the long-tested home remedies, but Divya did not get better; instead the fever continued and she had a nosebleed, which was most unusual for her. She had been a healthy child with hardly ever an ailment.

Her parents concluded it was time to take her to the family

physician, an elderly man of vast practical experience, though with no pretence to the latest technologies and specializations. He arranged for some basic blood tests while treating her for flu.

When the clinical reports came in, it was seen that her platelet count was low. Platelets are important in the process of blood clotting. A low count leads to small bruises bleeding profusely, or to the development of pinprick bleeds (patechiae). This was probably a factor in causing the seemingly unprovoked nosebleed.

The family doctor referred his patient to a paediatric specialist, who, after a physical examination and more blood work including cultures, believed Divya just had viral infection and treated her accordingly. The girl had taken a week's leave from school which was against her wont, but she accepted it with quiet resignation, and brightened up at the prospect it offered her to have frequent and, her state permitting, prolonged conversations with Ramana Thatha.

"Thatha," said Divya, softly breaking the silence of the morning, "why has God given sickness to human beings?" He did not reply immediately. After a while, he said, "Divya, if you had asked me why we get fever, or diarrhoea, or toothache, I could tell you the physical factors involved in such ailments. But you are asking a far deeper question, about the fundamental cause of sickness and its role in life and learning. It calls for a longer and deeper explanation, starting with basics. Eat your porridge and we will talk."

"You are right about the question I asked, Thatha," said Divya. "I was not thinking of my fever and cold. I want to know why we were created in this way. And why did God create sickness and unhappiness? You have always taught me that there is a rightness to everything. I want to see that in the total scheme of life."

And she dutifully ate her porridge, more from a desire to be free to listen to a topic that fascinated her.

Thatha began his narration, step by step, recalling the exposition of the sages who were the scientists of life. Unlike the scientists of the material world, these sages had vision that fully unravelled the workings of both mind and matter. "All of us are have both mind and body. The body is inert – by itself, the body cannot have any of the properties of a live person. These properties are, as you know, Divya, the ability to see, hear, taste, touch and smell, which are the respective functions of eye, ear, tongue, skin, and nose. These five are called the organs of knowledge or *jñānendriyas*, because it is through these five 'doors' that our mind receives all knowledge of and contacts the external world.

"Think of how many of these organs you are using in even the simple act of eating porridge! Each of us constructs our knowledge of the world from the data collected through these organs. This is the way the world enters our consciousness, stays therein as memory, gets formatted into desires and demands interaction for fulfilment thereof.

"Now, to be able to interact with the external world, each person is endowed with five organs of action, *karmendriyas*, and these are: feet for walking, hands for grasping, voice for communicating, and the organs of procreation and excretion. We enter the world with these and transact with it through them.

"Our quest for abiding happiness drives our life energy, day after day, year after year, into perception, desire, action and reaction. Such activity demands harmony between our consciousness and our body, between mind and matter. There has to be a matching of energy and equipment, a fine-tuning of the machine to run on the fuel."

He paused. Divya's face showed she had no difficulty in grasping the meaning of his words. "I can see that, Thatha. Our mind receives the information inflow, stores it, and shapes our activity based on it. This interaction is the flow of life."

"Good girl!" Thatha applauded encouragingly. "Now let's understand how consciousness works. All our activities stem from three *guṇas* or modes of mind: *sattva, rajas,* and *tamas.* The pure, calm, clear and virtuous nature in us is the *sattvic* mind; the roused, turbid, active and dynamic aspect in us is the *rajasic* mind; the dark, dull, selfish and lazy tendencies come from the *tamasic* nature in us.

"Every personality is a mixture of these three, but the proportions vary. The dominance of *sattva* makes a person wise and loving; more *rajas* results in a leader and achiever; and too much of *tamas* could make you lazy, evil, or dull. Do you follow so far?"

Divya nodded.

"Good. As I was saying, the functions of the mind must match the structure of the body in each person at every moment. And the outcome of their merger is what we call the personality or psyche of the individual. The physiological life in us is called *prāna,* divided into five vital airs or *pañcha-prāṇas.*

"*Prāṇa* regulates our circulation, digestion and respiration. Each of the three *guṇas* of the mind has a dominant interaction with one of these physical systems. To maintain the balance between mind and body so that we function true to our individual nature, any change at the *guṇas* or mental level demands a corresponding change at the *prāṇa*-complex or physical level. The joint changes restore the overall balance of the body-mind amalgam.

"Changes in our body functions are thus the natural responses to causal changes in our mental make-up. Our body is inert by itself and cannot get fever or catch a cold or develop a boil, unless a change in the energy-flow of our pervading consciousness demands such a change in our body. A rock or a table cannot get a fever or a cold; there is no consciousness flowing as energy in the stone or table."

Divya, all attention so far, now asked, "But, Thatha, we read in class that changes do take place in matter. Rocks in a river erode, and boulders heated by the sun for centuries may get fragmented. Even soil, tossed about by wind and water, can be changed chemically into a new form. What is the function of the *guṇas* or the mind in this?"

Ramana Thatha said, "A valid question, Divya, but it contains its own answer. Are the rocks and the soil aware of the changes they have been subjected to? Are the floods and the raging winds aware of the changes they have wrought? Is there any knowledge or feeling in them?

"The question about the role of the mind in this case has been raised by you, a conscious person, and not by the elements. We have been discussing the role of the *guṇas* in the mind-body amalgam of a living person, not in insentient bodies. So there is no contradiction. Change can be recognized only where the *guṇas* function, and that is in consciousness.

"I will not go into more detail now, Divya. Understand just this much: that all changes in the body complement changes in the mind. It is one integrated system and the energy for change can only be initiated in the consciousness.

"At the body level, we call some of these changes 'sickness'. They can be caused by stress, anger or fear – all qualities of the mind. Before these factors manifest as our actions in the world outside, they have already manifested as the disturbed *guṇas* in our consciousness, and hurt our body."

Ramana Thatha looked at Divya's pensive face and stopped. "My dear Divya, I hope I haven't bored you with all this heavy talk?"

"No, Thatha, I find it fascinating, and I am glad you spoke about all this to me. I understand now that my present sickness is caused by such undercurrents in my mind, and not by the anger of God. I will try to understand this causation deeper. Is this what they call Karma, Thatha?"

"Yes, child, this is what they call Karma."

❧

8

A week passed, yet Divya's health was not back to normal. She had always been a healthy and active girl and this sudden advent of many deficiencies and discomforts, continuing and multiplying over several days, was by now a cause for alarm. In addition to fever and cough, she had fairly severe pain in several bones of her body. There was noticeable weight loss, pallor in her usually rosy cheeks, and poor appetite. She seemed fatigued and one could sense an overall wasting of her body. She would sweat at night and it was not due to the weather.

There was thus ample cause for consternation in the family. Her father, Govinda, tried to return from his office earlier and also to avoid travelling on business, so that he could provide comfort to Divya and strength to his worried wife. Any change in Raman, the grandfather, was difficult to fathom, for as they say, still waters run deep, and it follows that deep waters are still. His silence and quietness hid the contents of his mind. In his eyes was a distant look – were they only trying to see things yet unseen? Or were they actually looking, through the folds of time, at a future beyond the horizon?

So it was back to the family doctor who referred them this

time to a paediatric oncologist of repute. Getting an early appointment in the busy schedule of the specialist was itself an ordeal, but an earnest request from the senior family doctor took care of that. Two days later, Divya, tired yet agile and alert, found herself ushered through the frost-glass door that proclaimed the occupant of the room beyond to be 'Dr. Shankar, Paediatric Oncologist'.

Dr. Shankar was a pleasant man with just such a ready smile as has been adopted as a trademark by paediatricians who presume that a child's confidence can be bought with a smile. But that has not been said here to detract any merit from the good doctor, for he indeed had a friendly heart that cared for, and reached out to, his young patients. "Divya," he intoned, looking at the chart. "Do you miss being in school? Want to go back?"

"Yes, Doctor."

"You will soon. We will give you a good check-up and then you can be on your own."

"Thank you, Doctor."

Then, to the father, Dr. Shankar said, "I will write out some tests. We need the latest picture, on top of what you already have. I want to make sure her liver is not affected. And we need to check her WBC count – that is, of her white blood corpuscles. You will need to come back the day after tomorrow, by when I will have the results. Good day."

After asking Divya and her mother to wait for them outside the room and seeing them out, the father hesitantly stumbled over his words, saying, "Can it be… Doctor, can you confirm…"

The doctor cut in, gently but firmly. "Nothing can be said till all the reports are in. Let us not speculate. See you in two days."

With that, the family returned home. The elders had their

fears but they did not want the child to hear the 'C' word yet. That is why they had asked her to step out of the doctor's room, while the father braced himself to ask if cancer was suspected. Of course, the doctor had known that this question would inevitably be asked. Was he not asking himself the same question?

The next day, Divya sat close to her Thatha. Looking into his eyes, she asked "Thatha, do I have cancer?"

He was bewildered for a moment, but quickly regained his accustomed composure: "Why do you ask that, child?"

Divya replied: "You see, Thatha, I read what was painted on the doctor's door. I knew 'paediatric' but I did not know the other word. So, while Mummy was sitting in a chair, I walked up to the reception counter. A young lady was there. She was free, and I asked her, 'Ma'am, what is an oncologist?' She said, 'It is a specialist doctor who deals with cases of cancer.' I kept that in mind, and when we came home, I looked up 'cancer' in your Oxford dictionary, Thatha. It said cancer is a malignant tumour in the body. I thought I would ask you – what is malignant, Thatha? And do I have cancer?"

Ramana Thatha had never communicated with Divya the way most adults do with children, shielding them from the truth with cover-ups. Leave alone comfortable lies of convenience, he seldom resorted to even half-truths. He wanted her to be shown the truth at a level at which her growing mind could absorb it. He encouraged her contemplation of the deeper significance of reality, so that she would progressively learn to discard the lesser for the greater, the lower for the higher. That is how true knowledge affects an enquiring mind which thereby outgrows the impact of temporal events to question its own origin and its ultimate destiny.

At the moment, cancer was only a flitting shadow that was

crossing the anxious minds of the parents; there was as yet no real basis for such fears. But Ramana Thatha knew that his role in Divya's life had to be beyond the influence of both hope and fear; he had to instil in Divya a basic understanding of the rightness of the play of Providence.

Only with such an understanding can the human mind not question the cosmic dispensation through ignorant intemperance, but accept everything with wise equanimity. Denying themselves that ultimate balance of life, human beings suffer the imagined tyranny of a haunting fate, live in fear of loss or pain or decay or death. They carry the seeds of recurring dismay and disaster into a cycle of birth and death. Knowing the truth of one's own self is the remedy, and Thatha's only wish for Divya was that she should know this great truth.

So he said truthfully, "Divya, no doctor has said that you have cancer. You heard Dr. Shankar say that he wants your blood to be tested and the results will be known only after two days. The doctor does not know yet what your malady is. Let us all wait without anxiety. You have probably heard some talk amongst the elders at school about someone having cancer and you have felt from whatever you heard that it is a serious, possibly dangerous, disease.

"You have asked me what cancer is. Cancer is not just one specific disease; it is a group of diseases. There are a hundred different types, but all forms of cancer start because the normal processes of continuous renewal of normal cells in our bodies, whereby old, dying cells are constantly replaced by new ones, are disturbed, and abnormal cells are produced in an imbalanced, 'out-of-control' manner, through cell-division beyond the normal limits. These unnatural cells may invade, that is, intrude on adjacent healthy tissues and destroy them. The sick cells may also spread to other locations in the body. Such migration is called 'metastasis'. All these are malignant properties of cancer.

"Most cancers form a tumour; that is what the dictionary said. I have told you about malignant tumours. There are also tumours, that is, lumps of cells, which are not malignant; they are not invasive and do not spread within the body. They are called benign tumours and are easily dealt with medically. All cancers do not form a tumour. Cancer is not contagious, not at all."

Thatha fell silent. He was telling Divya all that could be of help to an intelligent person like her to cope with her ordeal in case she had cancer. It came to his mind to tell her that she need not necessarily deem it as an inherited condition, when he thought better of making such a banal statement about what is essentially a matter of profound wisdom. The physical and medical sciences, locked as they are within the material frame, do not truly appreciate the significance of inheritance.

Inheritance is not about the genes one inherits from one's parents. It is not about DNA or proteins, amino acids or any other molecules. All molecules are an assemblage of carbon, nitrogen, hydrogen, oxygen, calcium, sodium, chlorine, zinc, iron and so on and on – all atoms, all units of insentient matter, all inert and dead.

Inheritance spells consciousness, sentiency, responsiveness – life. Visible change is in matter; felt change is in the mind. When dead time becomes living memory, the continuity in experience is inheritance. Who is the donor and who the inheritor? Is there a twosome, the one and the other?

All of creation is one flow of causation, an unending, uninterrupted sequencing of cause into effect, and the effect is felt where the cause operates. Inheritance is therefore one's present manifesting out of one's own past. The parents inherit the child as truly as the child inherits the parents. There is never a giving which is not at once a taking in equal measure – only the coinage varies. So, in truth, one inherits oneself and creates the future inheritance for oneself. All is a play of consciousness.

When cancer happens, as when anything happens to the body, it is the play of one's own consciousness that provides the cause and the result; there are no genes that can initiate a mutation, and there is no divinity that interferes with the eternal flow of causation. The conscious psyche at the centre of the event is the initiator and the inheritor, the subject and the object of the experience.

The wise one is he who sees this inviolable law as the perpetual truth of all life and all events, and conquers destiny through such understanding. Oh Divya, thought Ramana Thatha, oh child of tender years, whatever be in store for you, may the essence of understanding of this divine methodology of life be instilled in you, and may it support you through all your trials.

"You have been far away for so long, Thatha," said Divya when Thatha's sight seemed to return to her. "What were you thinking?"

"Nothing that I haven't told you before, my dearest child, and nothing that I will not be telling you again. Now you rest awhile."

9

The family returned to Dr. Shankar and he was ready to talk to them. "We do not know anything yet for sure," he said in relaxed tones that invited confidence in his words. "We will check Divya for tumours through scanning. As far as we can see now, there do not seem to be any tumours. If one is found to be present, a tissue biopsy will be done.

"Remember that I am not talking of something threatening or disastrous. 'Cancer' is a word that the medical profession can handle with expertise, but it remains a word that causes instant fear and despair amongst laymen. I assure you that most cancers can be treated and contained; some can even be cured. The stage at which the patient is first brought to us is of paramount concern, and you have done well in coming for diagnosis at the earliest. There are malignant cancers and benevolent tumours.

"I am not belittling the health problem we may have on our hands, but I am saying all this so that you may not be too anxious and distracted by mere speculation. We will go with the facts. Now Divya has a mild disorder of the spleen. Her haemoglobin is too low. Her WBC count is higher than I like and I am concerned. Her platelet count is low. I mention this so that you understand that the blood profile is disturbed, and there must be specific reasons which should be isolated and treated.

"Now we will check Divya's basic parameters for the record and do some scanning. Then you may go home." Looking at Govinda, he said, "You may come to see me two days later, to review the progress, but Divya need not be brought in at that time, for I will not have to check her physically any more."

On the way home, the silence was loud, and Divya realized that with her rested the only chance of restoring near-normalcy. So she tried to make light of the heavy moment and said, "I do not feel bad or sick really. I am even a wee bit hungry. But they messed me up with all the scanning. Greasy stuff all over me and then wiped off with cotton wads, while I was craving for a bath!" She giggled, but the response from the others was weak. So she tried something else. "Thatha, what is a scan? Is it an X-ray?"

"There is a difference, Divya, though both give information about the inside of the body that is not visually accessible. But whereas X-rays outline only bones and some formations that are opaque to the light spectrum of X-rays, a scan reveals images of all the fleshy organs and even offers cross-sectional details of their interiors. It is a great tool of modern medical science."

"It must be, Thatha," agreed Divya, smiling, "though I wish they didn't grease me up so!" But, for all the brave front that the family tried to put on, a mist had descended upon their dawn and the men knew that it was not a single problem, but a basket of problems that had been placed upon their shoulders, though the outer wrappings were still intact and the exact contents still lay concealed.

Govinda and Raman made the next visit to Dr. Shankar, and were promptly ushered into his cabin. The air itself seemed dense and tense – or was it only their imagination? The doctor spoke solemnly. "I deal with similar cases day in and day out, yet it does not get to be any easier to talk to the parents. I have grown to like Divya personally. Though I am a professional, I too feel the agony; after all, we are all human.

"There is still a bright side. Medical science has a brilliant record of rapid and ingenious strides in treating cancer." A pause. Then: "Yes, I said cancer. Divya has no tumours and that is a relief, but she has blood cancer, known as leukaemia. It is no doubt a serious matter. Her condition is termed Acute Lymphocytic Leukaemia, ALL. The cancerous changes take place in a type of bone marrow cell that normally goes on to form lymphocytes, which are infection-fighting immune system cells. These cells are rendered ineffective, so immunity from infection is lost. The person becomes defenceless.

"Acute leukaemia is characterized by the rapid increase of immature blood cells. This crowding makes the bone marrow unable to produce healthy blood cells. Immediate treatment is demanded in such cases as the rapid production and accumulation of the malignant cells leads to their spilling over into the bloodstream. Then they spread to other organs of the body. With early treatment, as in this case, the survival rate, especially amongst children, is quite high. But who can predict?

"Now we have to hasten to admit the patient and start the procedures. I have had more than ten years of hands-on experience in this field and I have built up a team approach because, with today's technology and specialization, more than one specialist is required to focus on each case. I hope this will endorse your faith and confidence in entrusting the case to me.

"I am attached to two cancer-speciality hospitals of repute. Both are equally competent and equipped and staffed, but one has been designed for the richer clients who want the best in rooms and environment and luxuries, so it is much costlier, while the other is safe and satisfactory without being so expensive. I felt that I should admit Divya into the second.

"Even then, treatment of cancer can run into millions of rupees and you must be prepared for it. It cannot be helped because the medicines, materials and services are unavoidably expensive. I will tell you more of this as the need arises; for now, I want to convey to you that there is no exploitation, only a compulsion.

"Now you must return home and make your assessments, and arrange for the funds, for the treatment should not be delayed. Because leukaemia prevents the immune system from working normally, the patient is prone to infection. Nausea may be caused by enlarged liver or spleen. Neurological symptoms such as headaches can occur. Pinprick bleeds or sore spots on the skin may come up due to deficiency of platelets in the blood. All such complications have a common cause, so do not get distracted exploring reasons or remedies. Do not delay."

Govinda found his voice. "Thank you for your time and your care. We needed to be briefed because we've been caught unawares. Doctor, we are financially at best a middle-class family. You mentioned that costs can run up to millions. We are stunned. Please tell us more specifically what amounts we should be ready with, and on what probable time schedule." Govinda turned to his father, who merely nodded assent. A melancholy thought drifted silently through Raman: in the modern world, 'm' dominates as mind, matter, money, and medicine.

The doctor replied: "A necessary question, my friend. I am from the middle class too, and I understand these grass-root concerns. We will have to start Divya on chemotherapy, which means treatment through chemicals. But the intravenous injections given repeatedly and voluminously constitute a painful and disturbing process.

"Each cycle may last for five or six days, and in the first assessment, there may be three such cycles. More may follow after a longer break. Not only will Divya have to spend several days in special sterile isolation rooms in the hospital, but frequent visits for tests are essential even after each discharge.

"Lastly, my friend, you asked about the costs. Each cycle of chemotherapy and related treatment may cost in itself around four lakhs of rupees. Intensive care and isolation room costs add on to this. So I would indicate to you that you initially marshal twenty-five lakhs to cover three months. I must caution you, if bone marrow or cord-blood transplant becomes inevitable even after chemotherapy, you will need up to twenty-five lakhs more, at least. I am sorry, but I have confided in you honestly. Any more questions?"

How could there be, in the numbed mind of Govinda? Silently, he nodded to the doctor and reached for the door. If it had been the irrepressible Divya in his place, she might have giggled at the doctor and asked, tongue-in-cheek: "Which bank shall I rob?"

10

They did not have the luxury of time to think before acting – both had to be done simultaneously. How was Govinda to convey the information to Divya's mother? And how to Divya herself? Oh God! Oh child of tender years! What doubts will assail your mind, what pains will wrack your body, what scars will disfigure your pretty face! I will delve into all the savings I have, I will mortgage whatever I own, oh God, only leave a roof over our heads. I will work day and night, I will not break my word of honour, I will not forfeit a debt, only let me take care of my child. In this crisis, what is mine that is not hers? Others will help, I can borrow and I will surely repay. I will go to the chairman of my company, the good soul will understand. God, dear God, why did it have to be Divya?

Such were Govinda's thoughts as he and his father made their way home. Grief filled Raman too, but he did not dwell on it, he accepted it, became a witness to the tragic play that had just begun to unfold. He had not exulted in happier days; he was not going to despair when sorrow knocked on his door. They were two sides of the same coin, and the presence of one announced the arrival of the other in due course of time.

He would strive to see that Divya remained a witness to her own turbulent state, through her understanding of the cosmic order; suffer she must, and suffer she will, but oh God, let your grace give her the understanding that your love alone functions as our experience of life.

God has scripted cosmic justice and the fruits of action evolve true to the seed that is sown. Is it lack of love if what is not deserved cannot be claimed? Or if what is due is never denied? *'Karturājñayāprāpyatephalam'* – action (Karma) yields fruit as the Lord has ordained that it should, declares Ramana Maharishi in *Upadeśa Sāram*, the quintessence of spiritual instruction. There is no undue favour or unfair prejudice in the operation of the cosmic law. That is total justice and therefore that is total love. O Lord, let Divya hold your hand with this faith.

When they reached home, Geeta was at the door, her face creased with anxiety. Divya had fever and nausea, so she was resting.

Govinda told his wife, "Let us prepare to shift Divya to intensive care at the hospital in which Dr. Shankar is reserving a bed for her. Pack up a few clothes for her and you get ready to stay at the hospital for about a week in the first instance. Then there may be a break, but we will have to go back again. She may be having a condition of blood cancer, but it is not too serious. With prolonged treatment, she will return to normal health. I know it is difficult, but worry will only make matters worse." He held her hand. "Geeta, let us be brave."

"Can we afford the treatment? What will we do?"

"I have worked it out. We can afford it. Leave it to me. Now you organize the domestic arrangements. I will go in and see Divya."

He found Divya propped up on the pillows. "How is my darling"?

"Could be better, daddy, but I can manage. What next,

daddy?"

"You need to be admitted as an in-patient, Divya. Your blood is not pure and you need transfusions and strong medication. Such chemical therapy is called chemotherapy."

"I know, daddy. It is a treatment for cancer."

Govinda held his composure with difficulty. "It is a related problem, yes, but not anything to worry about, Divya. But the treatment is prolonged till a complete cure is achieved. You must bravely put up with it."

"I will try, daddy."

Govinda got ready briskly and left for his workplace. The factory he worked in specialized in the fabrication of large reaction vessels, centrifuges and compact pharmaceutical plants. They worked with special alloys that had been developed under the initiative of Govinda and this had given them an edge over their competitors.

The chairman virtually owned the factory and managed it competently, being adept at finances and administration. Govinda was one of the technical pillars of his company, besides being a trusted lieutenant who protected for his boss the metallurgical secrets so vital to their prosperity.

Above all, the chairman was a good human being who held Govinda's family in respect. He had spoken to Divya at some social get-togethers at the factory, and had special affection for her. Who hadn't!

It was late afternoon and there was no pressure at their workplace. The chairman could give Govinda all the time he wanted. "Something special? What is it, Govinda?" And Govinda narrated the whole episode.

The chairman was quick to grasp the import of what was

being said. "You will need to deposit a sizeable amount before they even admit Divya, that is the way hospitals function these days. Govinda, I will be glad to give you right now a gift of two lakhs from the company. In addition, I will sanction a loan of three lakhs which can be recovered from your salary in easy instalments.

"Let me use this occasion to inform you that the factory's general manager is getting superannuated in two months and the board of directors has more or less decided to promote you to that post. I am happy. Is it not a strange fact of life that sorrow and joy walk up the same street often and we do not know who is coming round the corner?

"Anyhow, let this impending elevation in your service be some comfort amidst the tight situations you are facing. I will stand by you during your trial. Let us pray for Divya's early recovery."

Govinda let his tears flow unabashed. This was more than he could have rightly expected. The treatment process could commence immediately due to his chairman's generosity. He would attend to future demands as they arose. Various options and hopes fluttered in his mind like fireflies on a dark night, but even that was enough now.

It is said that a water-beetle walks on water, but should it stop to ponder how it is walking on water, seemingly against all laws of gravity, it would sink right there! Govinda only knew that he was afloat today and he would keep walking into the impossible. He thanked the chairman and got up to leave.

The chairman said kindly, "Do not be worried about work here. Come when you can and go back as you wish. You may be needed full-time there on several days. Divya is our top priority. All the best, Govinda."

11

While her father was away at the factory, Divya decided she would use the time to talk to her grandfather about a question that was taking shape in her mind. She saw that her mother was busy choosing clothes and packing them, and could sense what was afoot. She called out feebly, "Thatha," and the answer came "Right here, child," as Thatha stepped into her room and sat in a chair by the cot.

Divya stepped down from the cot and sat down on a floor-rug near Thatha's feet. She liked to do that because, as Thatha spoke to her of deep matters, she could rest her head upon his knees and listen intently. She felt that, just as the sound of his voice entered through her ears, a soul-current of subtle thought entered her through the physical contact, enriching her understanding. "Thatha, daddy told me that I should be prepared for prolonged treatment at the hospital, and should endure it bravely. I thought he was indicating to me that the process would be painful. Thatha, what is pain? And how does one endure pain?" Her head nestled closer as she awaited the reply.

Thatha put his hand on her shoulder. He was in a reverie and therefore silent. He knew the truth of God's creation. Pain was of the body, not of consciousness. It was a thing known to the consciousness, one amongst the many things known to it. Pain was a mechanical device integrated with our physical body so that the structure of flesh and bone would not be stressed beyond endurance and unwittingly damaged. It was a protective device to alert us in time to do whatever was possible to restore safety.

But suffering is different from physical pain. Unlike pain, it is in the mind, and not an unavoidable physical consequence of whatever had disturbed the body's physiology. But the human psyche habitually believes that body and mind are an amalgam, and, unless awakened to the underlying truth, automatically 'suffers pain'.

Raman was seeing in memory the words of philosopher-poet Kahlil Gibran in *The Prophet.* When asked to explain what pain is, the same question that Divya had now asked him, the poet had said: "Watch with serenity through the winters of your grief. Much of your pain is self-chosen. It is the bitter potion by which the physician within you heals your sick self. Therefore trust the physician, and drink his remedy in silence and tranquility. For his hand, though heavy and hard, is guided by the tender hand of the Unseen. And the cup he brings, though it burn your lips, has been fashioned of the clay which the Potter has moistened with His own sacred tears."

What lofty thoughts! The poet was straddling the majestic peaks of spirituality, and laying bare, in beautiful words, the vision his high perch revealed. That was the truth of pain: not a discomfort grudgingly borne, but the concealed gift of reunion with the source.

To know this would be to know the place of death in the scheme of life. But how would he be able to convey it to Divya, briefly, rapidly, vividly? For that was the need of this perplexed moment. Divya, possessing an intensity and wisdom far beyond her tender years, had been somewhat prepared already, but he must touch her soul now. So he began to speak. "Pain is the ringing of alarm bells in the physical system, Divya, to alert you to the rising stress and strain in the protesting organ of the body. Then you give it rest, relief and nourishment, medicines as necessary, and it recovers. Pain cannot be avoided but it can be accepted in terms of cause-effect rightness that you know so well. Unwise eating brings on stomach ache; overstraining your legs and arms causes muscular pain, meddling with the ear gives you earache.

"The pain should be accepted, as it is natural in that state. To feel aggrieved that there is pain is to rebut the natural law and that serves no purpose, but the erroneous mind that protests unfairly suffers. You asked how one can endure pain. It is not endured through denial, but through acceptance. It is endured when you do not enlarge physical pain into mental suffering.

"You are not the body, Divya – you are not flesh, bone, blood and brain. You are the energy of consciousness pulsating in the body equipment, as electricity in a bulb. You are the light in the bulb, and pain is a resistance in the circuit which produces wasteful heat and dims the illumination. Health is the restoration of normal voltage in the bulb."

Divya's eyes widened on hearing this scientific analogy from her Thatha and she smiled as she understood its meaning.

"Remember, Divya, electricity was not born when the bulb was invented. Your body has its birthday, but you don't. As consciousness, you are timeless, but, as Divya, you have one lifespan. Believing totally that you are the body is the great original ignorance. Your body was formed from matter, and named 'Divya', and you learnt to believe and to repeat 'I am Divya', but what is speaking is not the body of matter, but the consciousness possessing the body the same way an object is owned. Through causal connectivity and continuity, this individualized consciousness is expressed as a personal psyche, with its passing joys and sorrows, desires and efforts, success and failure, stress and strain.

"As I have told you before, disease is mental disharmony reflected in the body as physical imbalance." Thatha paused, patting Divya's head lovingly. "The need has come, Divya, for you to stand apart from your bodily identification, and to be, as far as possible, a witness to the physical alterations. The causes so far lying unmanifest in your past will now manifest as cancer with all the attendant pain. Cause must flow into effect. When it has flowed out fully, your ordeal will be over, child. Till then, see only the caring hand of God behind everything. Remember that divine grace has to operate as punishment sometimes, like a mother has to slap her child sometimes.

"And when I talk about the original ignorance, it is not your personal 'ignorance' I am talking about, Divya, but an aspect inherent in creation. Many go through life, even several lives, without ever knowing about it, but I have learned of it and now you have heard it from me. Make it your first priority to rise above it, Divya, to revolt and declare, every moment: 'I am not the body. I am pristine consciousness'. Our scriptures have declared *'na jātō na mṛto'si tvaṃ na te dehaḥ kadācana'* – 'You are not born nor do you die. At no time do you have a body.' What more needs to be said?"

Ramana Thatha stroked the head upon his knees. Those pretty tresses of hair would soon be sacrificed to chemotherapy and gasps of pain would wring her body, there was no help for that. But let her spirit stand up and remain detached and proclaim its valiant victory over flesh, he prayed. "Have you been listening, child?" he asked.

Divya lifted her head and looked into his eyes. "Every word, Thatha, every word. My heart is beating to a new refrain." She put her head down again and grandfather and grandchild slipped into the peace of light slumber, tired but empowered.

❧

12

The admission into the hospital was meticulously organized after rupees three lakhs had been remitted and recorded as the initial payment up front. Clinical tests and instrumental probes and non-invasive observations were all unhesitatingly ordered by Dr. Shankar with the quiet authority of a man who is sure of himself. Only the mother was permitted to stay with Divya; the others said the sweetest words with the saddest tone and withdrew, knowing future visits would be strictly monitored.

In the lobby, Dr. Shankar caught up with them. He said to them, "It is said that the darkest hour of the night is just before dawn. When Divya was diagnosed with cancer, that was merely the darkest hour. Dawn will break."

"God willing," said Raman, "let it be so."

"We are grateful to you, doctor," said Govinda.

Niranjan said nothing. The situation had not quite sunk in yet for him, though he felt there was a lurking anxiety. In what sense was the darkest hour lingering in their midst? The three walked out of the hospital.

Dr. Shankar had projected a five-day course of chemotherapy as the first cycle of treatment. Chemotherapy is an attempt to eliminate through drugs all cancer cells in the body, or at least control the growth and spread of these life-threatening cells to relieve pain and to prolong and enhance the quality of life vouchsafed to the patient. It is often a combination of several drugs that work together to kill cancer cells.

The doctor's experience and, one may say, intuition form a major factor in deciding upon, and progressively varying, the combination of drugs, taking into consideration the stage and grade of the cancer, the patient's age, and tolerance towards treatment and side effects.

The side effects constitute the great distress caused by this treatment. There can be hair loss, mouth sores, nausea, vomiting, diarrhoea or constipation, fatigue and loss of appetite. The liver may suffer damage. In spite of all this, if chemotherapy saves and prolongs life, where is the choice but to opt for it? The price has to be paid.

Chemotherapy is usually administered in cycles, the drugs being taken daily or weekly for a period of several months, with a brief recovery period after each cycle, when the body can rest and hopefully produce new, healthy cells. The drugs in chosen combinations are usually given intravenously, allowing rapid distribution through the bloodstream in the entire body. This needs special care because the strong medication can cause damage to surrounding tissues like muscles, nerves and skin if the medicines exit from the veins.

Apart from peripheral veins in the hands, veinous access may be through central veins like the internal jugular or femoral vessels, which are large in size and can be used for long chemotherapy schedules. Sometimes, to overcome the constraint of poor peripheral veins, a port is inserted into the body, and needs to be retained for frequent cycles of treatment.

For Divya, it was suspected that there had been damage to her bone marrow. Normal bone marrow cells were displaced by grossly higher numbers of immature white blood cells, resulting in a lack of blood platelets, which are vital to the process of blood clotting. She was prone to develop pinprick bleeding and, if bruised, could bleed profusely.

Further, in her present state, healthy white blood cells, which are involved in fighting pathogens, could have been suppressed or rendered dysfunctional. This could cause her immune system to be unable to fight off a simple infection. It could even cause her immune system to start attacking other healthy cells, so that, in an ironic twist of nature, the saviour becomes the savage, the protector becomes the pestilence.

Therefore, the risk of infection was now at its worst. The excessive number of dysfunctional white blood cells interfered with the level of other cells and caused a harmful imbalance in the blood count. For all these reasons, the strictest regime had to be enforced to protect Divya. This tender girl in the fifteenth year of life was evidently destined to endure severe and prolonged physical trauma for months or maybe even years to come.

There would be the nurses, trying to look kind and act gentle, feeling the arms for a receptive vein – "Just a prick, my dear, you won't even feel it!" – but then several such injections per day of high-dose multi-drug treatment would follow, with the right and left arms poked alternately till they were blue and sore, and finding a vein for the next injection became tricky, even vexatious.

Divya held out her arm mechanically – "Clench your fist, Divya" – I will, she told herself, but I will not clench my teeth;

after all, it is only an injection, and I am not the body, I am pristine consciousness. Yet … ouch! it hurts, it is where the arm has been poked already and therefore that much more painful. But I am supposed to witness the pain. That is the truth and Thatha has injected these ideas already into my mind! She laughed feebly at her own humour.

Her mother looked up and asked, "Did you say something, my little one?"

"I just said, mummy, that you should go out and have your food."

"Oh, I will do so by and by, but now you can have some boiled vegetables and toast, then a little fruit and custard."

"Nausea makes it difficult, mummy, but I will try fruit and a little hot milk."

Tomorrow will be the same, and the day after will be the same. Cause-effect, cause-effect, all the way. I must remember that constantly, said Divya to herself, and then no questions will remain awaiting an answer. Residual causes in my life's history, their origins now unknown to me, are manifesting as cancer in my body. That is the cause for the medication. And medication is the cause for my discomfort.

But bodily discomfort is not an inevitable cause for mental distress. I must live with it. Only another three or four days, then there will be a break. Thatha would expect me to take it quietly, a day at a time.

The first cycle of chemotherapy lasted six days. The onset of leukaemia had been rapid in this case, calling for drastic treatment straightaway. Blood transfusions had to be given, along with booster injections, and, for hours at a time, Divya had to lie flat on her back, basically immobilized.

Then Dr. Shankar came to say with assumed cheer: "Divya,

you are a great patient! You are getting better and so I will send you home for a few days. You can be quite normal, even go to school for a while and meet your friends and teachers, but do not strain too much, and if you feel sick, tell your parents immediately. I will call you back after five or six days."

"Yes, doctor. I need to feel stronger, though."

13

F ive days later, Divya was called back to the hospital. She looked a little better due to the respite she had had from daily doses of strong medicines like Vincristine, Prednisone, and Daunomycin, and other oral steroids. These drugs are not target rifles handled by sharpshooters who pick out the victim with immaculate aim, but, rather, rapid-fire machine guns that sweep the suspected territory, bringing down the culprits, no doubt, but with them many an innocent bystander too. Not only are the cancer cells progressively eliminated, but many healthy cells get affected too, causing the distressing side-effects.

But there is no option and the treatment must continue till all the errant cells are destroyed. If there are ten thousand cancerous cells and all but ten of them are successfully eliminated, those ten can multiply or migrate within the body and colonize in other organs, threatening life again as much as before the treatment started. That is why several cycles of chemotherapy are necessary.

Divya was back in the sterile zone, her mother the only one to keep her company, back with the smiling sisters in their starched and spotless dresses shuffling in and out on silent feet, back to the sharp needles cajoling the shrinking veins to permit entry. The recent blood profile had been cause for concern, the platelet count was low, and she was having difficulty walking because of the pain in her bones. The doctors attending on her let it be known that after five or six days of chemotherapy this time, she may be required to stay on in the ward, to facilitate monitoring as she was so prone to infection and not the slightest risk could be taken.

In accordance with protocol, the accounts department of the hospital sent an official demand note to Govinda that a payment of rupees five lakhs should be made forthwith. A bill was enclosed for expenditure incurred so far, which Govinda read through blinking eyes and it slowly sank in on his unbelieving senses that the total exceeded the three lakhs he had paid in advance by no less than another fifty-five thousands. The drugs were so expensive, the exclusive accommodation by itself was like being in a five-star hotel, and the 'special diet' prescribed for a charge and wheeled in for a fortune, whether consumed or not, added significantly to the costs.

The shape of things to come was now more clearly visible to Govinda, and he knew that there is no substitute for money but money. He made his own projections and could estimate that the complete routine of chemotherapy over four or five cycles, and the hospitalization would surely cost no less than twenty-five lakhs. He must plan to raise this amount over the next three months. Can one put a price tag on life, and that too, on the life of one's fifteen-year-old daughter?

It would mean the end of all his savings, and the selling of all his liquid assets. He would have to go into debt in a large way, if borrowings could be obtained. His most troubling thought was how he would manage without being compelled to sell his home, the one essential security for the future. Oh God, would he have to make a choice between a roof for Divya's head and a roof for Divya's life? Was not the answer self-evident? But what of Niranjan, what of Geeta?

No, he said to himself, this is not the way to think; it is but the way to sink. I can raise the money. Let me start with a visit to my bank. The manager is as helpful as he is efficient. And he has a good opinion of me, my career, and my values. But why am I getting agitated now? There is time. I still have two lakhs from what the chairman gave me. I can take three more from my own funds. That will give me at least ten days to consolidate my position.

Govinda remitted five lakhs into the hospital account, reassured Geeta, reviewed the situation briefly with his elderly father, and decided, in consultation with him, to call for a gathering of the larger family, that is, of his two brothers and their spouses included. The reunion was fixed for the following Sunday, two days away.

Making and serving lunch for all would be difficult in the circumstances, so they would meet for evening tea. Geeta would take time out from being with Divya for a few hours. Niranjan was there with all his cousins, but Divya, who was always the one to spark off the gaiety, was not, and the mood was sombre, the greetings hesitant, and a heavy pall lay over the home.

Govinda told them how exactly matters stood, medically and financially. Raman broke the ensuing silence with his soft and soothing voice. "This is our long hour of trial," he said, addressing Govinda's brothers, "a period when our character and our courage are tested. I have no doubt our family is bound by ties of genuine affection and caring. The burden of today is too vast for one man's shoulders; heart-strings and purse-strings must be loosened.

"But who might do exactly what is not an easy equation to write. The times are such that survival in the competitive world demands intellectual excellence and the clout of money equally. Owning a decent house and a good car, providing for higher education, a marriage, or even an adequate wardrobe, plans for entertainment, social obligations, or an annual holiday – even one of these would dent one's savings. Above all, one has to save continuously, these days, for the education of the children; you have two children each, bright, by God's grace, and naturally ambitious. You have to think of their future and provide the most you can for them.

"The poet-philosopher says, 'There are those that give and know not pain in giving, nor do they seek joy, nor give with mindfulness of virtue; they give as in yonder valley the myrtle breathes its fragrance into space. Through the hands of such as these God speaks… It is when you give of yourself that you truly give.' So, I say to you, do not consider yourselves bound by obligations, for love has no impositions, it is free. Take your time to think it over, consult amongst yourselves, and in a few days, speak about it to Govinda."

Ravi and Sekhar exchanged glances, then each looked at his wife. Heads were nodded ever so gently; Sekhar leaned towards Ravi's ear and mumbled softly, and Ravi nodded assent.

Sekhar addressed his father: "Father, as always your words guide us through every crisis with worldly wisdom coupled with spiritual insights. We will think further on the lines you have so beautifully and truthfully laid down for us. Yet, we can straightaway indicate the immediate support we can extend to help care for our beloved Divya. Ravi and I will give, with our love and prayers, two and a half lakh rupees each. We can afford to do so by drawing on our savings, without disturbing our ongoing needs. We hope we are enabled by the Lord to extend further support as the need arises."

Govinda's eyes turned moist and he could not speak. Geeta mumbled, "How fortunate we are to have brothers like you," and her sisters-in-law put fond arms around her.

Raman said, "Such has been God's will, now revealed through your words. This is how it should be with brothers, and the love shared will be a blessing shared."

They tried to lighten the moment, for love just as much as grief lays claim to the heart; both gratitude and betrayal numb the mind on first impact. So they all moved around for the sake of moving, and the ladies gave it purpose by getting ready to make and serve tea.

That done, Ravi and Sekhar had another weighty subject to disclose, and now was the time for it. Their family priest had recently visited both their homes and spent some time talking to the men, who were office-bound, and much more time talking to the ladies, who had no other option. He had been at great pains to emphasize the urgency of his duty, no less at this hour of mighty upheavals in Govinda's family.

He had Divya's horoscope with him, and as soon as he had heard of her serious illness, he had rushed to his brother-in-law than whom there was no greater astrologer in the neighbourhood, why, in Chennai itself, why, anywhere, and consulted him. They had both agreed that various poojas and *homams* must be undertaken immediately to propitiate the *devas*, and some pilgrim centres visited. He was aware that Geeta was virtually all day at the hospital and wanted a time to be fixed for him to meet them both at home. The great astrologer had also kindly consented to accompany the priest.

Govinda looked askance at his father. Raman said, "Let the priest come on Tuesday, that is, the day after tomorrow, at ten in the morning. Geeta will be here with Govinda. I will be here too." Then he added, "We should not refuse the priest's request. Tell him the astrologer's visit can be kept for another day."

As they got ready to depart, the sisters-in-law told Geeta that, as a lengthy period of hospitalization was now evident, they would take turns staying with Divya whenever Geeta wished. On that note they parted, driving into the distant sunset.

❧

14

Shastrigal, the family priest, came in riding his motorbike at 10 a.m. on Tuesday, bedecked in a heavy gold chain round his neck, precious earstuds, and traditional marks of sacred ash and vermilion on his forehead. He was received with demonstrated respect as due to him and was seated ceremoniously. He accepted the proffered silver tumbler of coffee.

"Who can predict the ways of God and who can protest against them? But God in His gracious compassion has also given us three weapons to overcome the tribulations and ill health that the body must face in its lifetime: *maṇi*, the valuable gems whose hidden powers of protection are much higher than their visible lustre or richness; *mantra*, the powerful Vedic chants whose meanings and vibratory forces can restore the body's lost harmony; and thirdly, *aushadham*, the herbal and mineral inheritance we have from nature's secret and sacred resources.

"Our child Divya, unfortunately, has had this unholy disease attacking her body at this tender age. The fault is in her stars, and therein lies the remedy too. Let the western-educated doctors play their role, and you can judge their efficacy over time, but armed with *mani, mantra,* and *aushadham,* let us pay our homage to celestial powers, and surely the child's health will be restored.

"I will organize, on your behalf, the *yajñas* and *homams* that will pacify the planets, distance the evil forces, and plead with death to accept our offerings and return our child to us. My brother-in-law, the famous astrologer of whose renown you must all be aware – who is not? – will cooperate with me wholeheartedly to guide us and even accompany us to the temples to be visited and on the pilgrimages that Govinda and Geeta, in particular, must undertake. We need to rightly identify and know the presiding deities of our destiny, and they will be propitiated when contacted in accordance with *Āgamaśāstra.*

"Furthermore, he will instruct you on the precious stones you need to wear on your fingers, wrists, or neck; their cost, though seemingly high in today's inflated market, is a trifle when compared to the power and protection they bestow upon the wearer. And, of course, you will be liberal as befits your status in giving gifts to the *archakas* who, led by me, will perform the *japa* and the *homams.* I need not tell an esteemed Brahmin family like yours that *go-dāna, suvarṇa-dāna, bhūmi-dāna* and *vastra-dāna* are considered mandatory. We will be a team of eleven Brahmins for the poojas, apart from the astrologer."

Geeta was sobbing. "I will do anything. Only save my child; by any means, save my child." Govinda might have sobbed too, but for a totally different reason. As it was, he was feeling realistically that he may have to sell the shirt off his back to meet the hospital bills. They were praying at the local temple, and their fervent pleas had of course been addressed to the Lord, whom they acknowledged as the ultimate saviour. But now the inescapable cross of fear and tradition was being laid upon them in the form of professionalized spirituality, which could neither be denied nor accepted easily. How far could they go and at what cost?

He knew Geeta's heart, head, and soul. In the given situation, they would not be different from those of many other mothers of a comparable family background. Her emotions would block practical decisions. Fear would drive her to desperate compliance, and any refusal would be seen in her aching heart as sacrificing her precious child, who could be saved, if only … if only … and was that too much to ask?

Shastrigal was waiting for their assent. Govinda had to reply. He said, "You are gracious. Your words are full of wisdom, learning, and good intent towards us. We will ponder over your words and decide what we can do. If we could, we would act on all your proposals. Our only problem is how we can afford further costs. The treatment and hospitalization is unbelievably expensive. Estimates for the course now being implemented are twenty lakhs. We do not have even that. We do not know which way to turn."

The holy man raised a palm in blessing. "The merciful *Īśvara* who gives you twenty will not deny you another two or three. Trust Him and set your priorities right."

It was now left to the eldest, Raman, to put the matter in the right perspective. "All that our Shastrigal has said has merit in it. We must reinforce the physical with the mental. While we do what seems rational by following medical advice and attention, we must also attune our mind with divine dispensation. The simple truth is that all is God's will and His doing. Though we are right in saying that all is God's will, how can we really know of any will other than our own? I can honestly say that it is my will to perform a certain action at this time, but how can I say that God is willing me to do this action?

"Therefore, we have to live with conscious honesty, trust the promptings of our mind, and do what seems best to us. While owning personal doership, we should be humble and honest, conceding that we seem to be agents acting in His name and by His command. Then we will not err by arrogating infallibility to our intellectual prowess.

" 'Thy will be done' is the perfect prayer, but folded hands have to become working hands. What befalls us in the causal continuity of our individual karma is the *prārabdha* or destiny that we have to face, and we cannot know in advance how the shuffled cards of causation will be dealt through the hand of Time." And Raman paused to think: Divya knows this, but none of you do.

He continued: "We have to play the game of life with the cards we receive and this becomes our *purushārtha*, the individual will translated to action on personal responsibility. Shastrigal, what you have said is true, but the ultimate Truth goes beyond that. It is true that the Vedas extol pooja, pilgrimage, and ritual. Men are led along these paths to approach the divine with *chitta-śuddhi*, purified minds.

"But becoming one with God, which is the ultimate goal and purpose of life, goes beyond. It begins where the 'I-am-this-body' idea itself is extinguished. The final declaration of our scriptures is:

Svarūpa-nirvāṇamanāmayo'ham

(I am free from disease – my form has been extinguished.)

"The individuality of the person is itself a mistaken notion, is in fact the primordial error of identity which makes a mystery of God and a reality of man, turning Truth upon its head. But we who speak and listen to this statement are ourselves the myth. Let the paradox be. It needs to be only indicated here, but beyond saying it, we have to function now as the persons that we are.

There is no escape.

"If we could mix the two streams of medical prescription and spiritual practices, we would do so, but large expenditure is involved. So availability of money and optimizing its dispensation is the limiting factor. Our known position today is that we can do the minimal essentials amongst the *homams*, which we certainly will, while we continue our customary prayers. Beyond that, time will reveal what must and can be done. The last word must be left to Govinda and Geeta."

The priest, familiar with this household through years of intimate association, got up and found his way to the toilet. Raman took the opportunity to caution the others. He said, "The actual expenses of what the priest suggests will far outpace the present indications. Travels to distant places, using taxis since pressure of time will restrict overnight sojourns, will cost dearly. The precious gems will consume our precious resources. Keep this in mind."

Shastrigal came out as Geeta moved into the kitchen. He walked in behind her. Their voices would not carry to where the two men were sitting. "Geeta," he said, with brotherly concern, "philosophy, when rationalized, gets lost in dialectics. It should stop its analysis at the threshold of vedic injunctions, which are beyond questioning. All that I have proposed has the sanction of the Vedas. The rituals, the incantations, the sequencing, the offerings – all must follow rigidly the ordained rules.

"Otherwise, not only may the fruits be negated, even contrary results may accrue. We priests are the intermediaries between God and the penitent petitioner, and only we know the channels of communication and interaction. Money is no doubt important, but we are without choice when the precious life of our child is in the balance."

"Oh God, oh God," mumbled Geeta, choked with grief, "save my child! Swami, save her."

"Not I, but the planets, and the deities who preside over our fate, will surely be the saviours, but you have to see to it that the proposals are implemented."

They returned to the living room. Prostrations betokened the traditional farewell, and the priest departed. It was time for Geeta to hurry back to the hospital.

❀

15

The days were passing, the weeks were passing. A second cycle of chemotherapy had been mercilessly imposed upon the tender frame of Divya, exhausted as she was. Her limp arms, with their shrunken veins, dreaded the prospect of more needles, but blood transfusions had to be administered, booster injections were prescribed, and the pain of the pricking was still the lesser part of the infliction. It was the nausea, the churning of her stomach, and the sheer weakness and helplessness that were the greater part of her suffering.

After a total of fourteen days of treatment, the blood counts were expected to show sure signs of recovery, but Divya's blood profile remained disturbing, and a lumbar puncture was necessary. This procedure would have to be carried out in the sanitized sanctuary of a surgical theatre, and the trespass into the secret crevices of the body by inquisitive investigators would demand its tribute of pain for hours to come. The insertion of a thick and long needle into the spinal column to extract the fluid necessary to study possible infection of the neural system would be excruciatingly painful. Poor Divya, already amply hurt, would have to bear this too.

With difficulty, the spinal fluid was extracted and clinically examined. The findings were not encouraging, though not disastrous, and left some hope that one more course of chemotherapy might reverse the negative trends. The patient was given three days to rest and recover before being subjected again to the heavy medication, but she had to stay on in the ward, being precariously susceptible to infections.

While such was the turn of events at the hospital, Geeta had wished for a Navagraha *homam* to be conducted at their house and she obtained the consent of her husband. The auspicious hour was fixed by Shastrigal, who arranged to collect the numerous prescribed items for the pooja, including *navadhānyāmśa,* the nine grains of seeds, the twigs of nine nominated plants, and the cloth pieces of nine colours associated with the nine planets to whom oblations were to be offered. The *homam* would be accompanied by *namakam,* the sacred worship of Lord Siva, and *chamakam*, the request for boons by the worshipper. And then there would be the offering of gifts to the priests.

The ritual was conducted accordingly, and the principled restraint of meek waiting could not quite conceal the eager anticipation of the priests for the bounty at the end. However, prudence could not allow the limits to be overstretched. Hybrid cows cost today what elephants cost in the old days for royal buyers. Still, mostly to satisfy Geeta, one good milch-cow with a young calf had been acquired, and that was gifted to the Shastrigal, after traditional *go-pūjā* (worship of the cow) had been done.

After that, emotion getting the better of reason, with tears streaming down her eyes, Geeta impulsively removed the pair of gold bangles from her wrists, bowed at the feet of the head priest, and handed them to him, sobbing "Save my child, save her!" The priest blessed her, saying, "Your generosity and your faith will not go in vain."

The other ten priests had perforce to be settled less generously, and were given a token two-gram piece of gold each. All were given clothes and rupees two hundred each; of course Shastrigal was handed one folded note of a higher denomination.

Thus ended the morning for Govinda, poorer in cash but richer in debt and richer in the promise of grace. His father was sitting alone in the verandah as Govinda went up to him. "Father, I am doing what I can," he said, feeling the need to say something, but not knowing how to make sense with words.

Raman saw the emptiness of the utterance, which was neither an informative statement nor an inquisitive question. He said indulgently, "It is neither necessary nor possible to have ready answers to many situations that trouble us in life. For, in the first instance, they are not questions, but facts of occurrence. It is the mind that turns facts into problems. Then the right answer is in how that mind sees it, and the action that follows is as that mind can decide. The mind itself is only memory, a repository of past experiences, conclusions, actions and reactions. A thoughtful mind wears tinted glasses; strangely, a thoughtless mind has a pure vision. But being unconditioned by thoughts does not mean a dull mind, for, at the same time, it must be an alert, observant mind. Carry on, son, as you are doing, but reflect on my words. The best that can happen to us will happen."

Govinda bowed to his father with folded hands and got up to take Geeta to the hospital and himself to the factory. On the way, Geeta informed him that she had fixed an appointment to meet the astrologer. She was convinced that she should perform Rahu pooja; many a miracle was credited to such worship.

Govinda said, "Yes. After that, we will leave it to God's mercy."

Geeta said, "The *devas* will respond. Our child will

recover."

At the hospital, as of now, the patient was not recovering. The team of doctors decided that a bone marrow test should be done. It would be a sensitive procedure, to be done under anaesthesia. The marrow would be aspirated from the breast-bone or the hip-bone. For Divya, there was a scant supply of marrow, which indicated that the marrow was getting depleted due to the onset of leukaemia. If it continued that way and turned critical, a transplant would be inevitable, and the only faint hope against such a contingency was that the next cycle of chemotherapy may reverse the trend and restore healthy marrow. A Hickman catheter was placed in her chest, to facilitate frequent, and sometimes prolonged, inputs of medication into her blood stream. Chemotherapy was started a day later. She was also put on continuous drip for three days.

When she was not dosed with the medications of chemotherapy, she received platelet and red blood cell transfusions and oral antibiotics. She had to take shots for her immune system and frequently blood was drawn for tests to monitor her functions. The torture of it all was a living hell which Divya had to endure and no amount of fortitude in a teenager could suffice to cope with such an ordeal. Yet there was no choice.

16

Govinda was seated in the privacy of his bank manager's imposing room, having been received warmly and shown the courtesy of being offered a cup of tea. Briefly and accurately, Govinda acquainted the manager with the facts of Divya's malady, the medical compulsions, the incurred costs and his financial resources so far, his own or borrowed or otherwise received.

"I see myself needing another ten lakhs to go through with what is in progress. If the treatment now envisaged suffices and if my child recovers from there on, this added amount should see us through. We hope it will be so.

"If, even after that, bone marrow transplant becomes the last resort, the added costs will be exorbitant. Then my only resource will be to mortgage my home, an unpretentious building in itself, but precious real estate.

"Now I am requesting you for a loan of ten lakhs on the strength of my executive salary, and assured service with my company for the next twenty years. My chairman has told me that I will soon be promoted as plant manager with a sizeable jump in my salary package. Therefore, I can pay any reasonable monthly instalment regularly and redeem the debt in the time frame you set."

The manager had the faintest smile on his face. He knew he had a good client and it would be a safe loan. "The proposal stands to reason," he said. "We will have to go through the motions of official evaluation of the request. Here is a set of forms you need to fill up – my secretary will assist you. I believe you can absorb into your budget an EMI – equated monthly instalment – of about fifteen thousand rupees. We will keep the interest as low as the rules and my discretion permit."

"Thank you, sir," said Govinda, moved by the liberal support. "I assure you I will honour my commitment."

A week later, the loan having been sanctioned, he cleared the fast-accumulating bills in the hospital. Then he went to see Dr. Shankar. The doctor's face foretold better news, as the dawn proclaims the coming sunrise. "Govinda," he said, "now we are seeing the revival we were working for. The WBC count is down and the RBC and platelet counts are coming up. These are signs of a remission, thank God!"

"And thank *you* too, Doctor," said Govinda, delight and relief bringing a tear to his eyes. "I will spread the news to the family."

"Be happy, Govinda, but guardedly so. Cancer may be manageable, but it is also unpredictable. We have to watch and be alert for months ahead. We will fight this together all the way. I have only done my duty in cautioning you. But go now, we have reason to feel happy today."

In the interim, Geeta had met with the astrologer in the hospital lobby itself and he had told her not to underestimate the importance of planetary dispensation upon their lives, and since the positions of the planets in Divya's horoscope were unfavourable overall, there was urgent need to pacify the planets through appropriate worship.

The first thing she should do urgently was to hasten to the *navagrahakshetras* situated around the town of Kumbakonam and do the poojas he would prescribe. He himself was otherwise tied down for that day and the next. So she would have to hire a taxi and go by herself, equipped with six thousand rupees for all the rituals. He would have his nominee meet her there and guide her through all the ceremonies.

Who can quantify the anxiety of a mother when her child is in a critical state? Go, said Geeta's mind, go and appease the planets. What will you do if tomorrow is a day too late? True, you have to be away from the hospital for one whole day, but that is to safeguard a lifetime.

Tears were her means of persuasion. She received her husband's dazed approval, for he had no scale by which to measure the merits of the deed. "Take Niranjan with you. He can miss school for a day," he said, and sent them off on the journey very early in the morning.

As they travelled, Niranjan said, "Ma, I hadn't known Divya's sickness was so serious, but now I understand. Are we going on this trip to pray for her life?"

"Niranjan, every prayer is for a better life, but sometimes it has to be for life itself. We are praying for Divya's recovery from cancer. She will get well soon, son, have faith."

"I will, mom. And I love Divya." It was late that night by the time the taxi brought them back home. The driver collected four thousand rupees and departed. Of the six thousand, only small change remained, but all the poojas had been completed to Geeta's satisfaction and there was respite.

Govinda met her at the portico. He reached out for her hand

and put an arm around Niranjan as he said eagerly, "Divya will be back home tomorrow. She is being discharged. Doctor says she has recovered."

Geeta clutched her husband's arm for support, swayed slightly and then steadied herself. "Merciful Lord, and blessed planets, you have heard this poor woman's prayers, you have saved my child."

Raman was standing by. They greeted him and walked into the house on wobbly legs, fighting the emotional upsurge. The night moved on unsteady feet, the morning was slow in coming.

To Raman's mind came a popular scriptural metaphor known as *'kāka-talīya-nyāyam'* which may be rendered loosely as 'the logic of the crow and the palmyra fruit'. The story goes like this: A crow comes flying and lands atop a palm tree. In that very instant, a fruit drops to the ground from the tree. The observer concludes that the settling of the crow on the tree has caused the falling of the fruit.

The question that arises is this: How can the two facts be related as cause and effect? Might it not be the case that the ripened fruit was ready to fall and indeed fell of its own accord, and it just happened that the crow sat on that tree at the instant the fruit was shedding its stem to drop down? If so, the two occurrences have simultaneity in time, but no causal connectivity. The conclusion is an error made by the observer who is guided by the superficial, not the substantial.

Applying the equation to Geeta performing the *navagraha poojas* and coming home to be told that the cancer has departed from Divya's body, it is easy to see how she concluded that the prayers had caused the miraculous healing. Would people not be justified in having their faith affirmed and heightened in such a way? Who is to confirm or deny the causal sequence in temporal terms of the worship and the remedy?

Raman knew the answer which indeed took the question itself to another plane before answering it, but who would understand it now? He hoped Divya would, in due course. For the present, he held his peace.

Divya came home before noon the next day, jaded and drowsy from all the sedation, still hurting from the jabs and just-removed tubes. Her aunt, who had been with her for the day that Geeta had been away, came with her.

Divya was moved into a room specially cleaned and scrubbed for her safety, and it was understood that she would be isolated and allowed to remain mostly alone, while she slowly picked up in strength. She was scheduled to visit the hospital once in four days for the present, and later she could see her family doctor once a week.

Family members and intimate friends had been duly informed and advised, so that there would be no crowding by well-meaning people. Yet all knew it would be a difficult and delicate regime to uphold.

For all her tiredness, Divya's face was suffused with joy, and love for all glowed in her eyes. She looked at Thatha, and Thatha looked at her, and sight held sight for a while, nothing being said, yet nothing remaining unsaid. For those moments, she was not aware of pain or even of time, and it dawned on her that a touch of the mighty truth of what she had been told earlier had revealed itself to her: "You are not the body, Divya, you are pure consciousness." Smiling within herself, she let her mind return to her surroundings.

17

A week passed by and Divya had become more stable. Like a passing shower on a sultry summer day, little moments of relief can in their time be a source of immense delight. So there was happiness in the household that had been so threatened by disaster. The fiscal demands that had to somehow be faced and resolved had no doubt left heavy burdens upon their frail shoulders, but they had not lost Divya, and the price paid in finance and forbearance, in agony and anxiety, did not matter at the moment because they dared to believe that Divya was saved.

After she had been given routine checkups at the hospital twice with intervals, they were told monthly checks would suffice thereafter, but they should be alert to any unusual symptoms. She could go to her school and even play games, but always avoiding strain, mental or physical.

So the rainbow was again back where it belonged, its graded pastoral shades a feast to the eyes, its graceful curves a symphony of sight. It seemed the whole neighbourhood was drawn unknowingly into the celebration, the sun of love within them emerging as light through eyes moist with relief, creating the rainbow that arched over their colony.

For Divya, the most significant aspect of this return to near-normal life was that she could be with Thatha as much as she liked, and Raman could find calm, undisturbed hours for communion with her. For her, the importance of such togetherness lay in the uplifting of her whole being into a rapture of self-discovery, an enchanting, empowering transportation into the reality of oneself, so hard to suspect unaided, but so apparent when revealed by Thatha.

For Raman, the importance lay in being able to act on the urgency he felt to convey to Divya the subtle truths of cosmic creation, of the Creator and the creature, of God and the person, without knowing which, nothing else had real meaning and worth. A lifetime of soul-searching for the ultimate Truth had enabled him to analyse and understand the answer. Though he laid no claim to the transcendental experience of self-realization, he knew that he possessed rightly what may be called self-knowledge.

Though he had, as the dutiful patriarch of his family, an equal involvement with each of its members, he knew in his wisdom that to all the others he could speak of morals and ethics and duties, to raise their values and make them better human beings, but his only prospect of guiding any one of them to go beyond temporal personality to godhood itself lay with Divya. God has been humanized, and the goal of life is that the human must be divinized.

Divya had been temporarily reprieved, but in his heart Raman knew that she was still in the shadow of death, for cancer lays a heavy hand upon its victim and does not easily relinquish its grasp. Therefore, the opportunity to communicate with her was too precious to be wasted. Who knew whether months or years remained? The mind set on achievement needs to treat each day as perhaps the last, and pour its energies into a frenzy of spirited dedication.

So it happened that Divya sought the cosy comfort of having Ramana Thatha's arm wrapped around her shoulder and then she began to speak. "Thatha, when I was not kept in total isolation in the hospital, I was shifted to the adjacent ward, where other cancer patients were also kept. I could hear what those next to me were saying. There was a boy, Kumar, who was of my age, and he too had cancer. He was often in pain and distracted.

"And then he would ask, sometimes in puzzlement, sometimes in agony, sometimes in the frustration of helplessness, he would sob or shout, 'But why me, ma, why *me*?' and his mother would say, 'God knows! I do not see what we have done to invoke this punishment,' and at other times she would say, 'I have done so many poojas, I have fulfilled my vows, and shall commit myself to more *vrathams* if you get well. Why is God so cruel towards us, son? What more can I do?'

"Thatha, I do not like to ask such a question. Because it will be like declaring, 'It should not have been me. It should have been some other person.' That is not right. And to say God is cruel is to be cruel to God, Thatha – how can we say such things? From what you have taught me, I can see that the answer to 'Why did Divya get cancer?' is, obviously, 'Because there were causes in Divya's life for which cancer in her body was the related and inevitable effect.' It could not be otherwise. It is the impartial law of causation at work. I see that.

"But, Thatha, I am unable to see the causal link in my own life. Where did I go wrong, Thatha? Where did I even unknowingly commit such a crime or error that this heavy price has to be paid? And look at what my condition is doing to all of you. What have all of you done – even you, Thatha – that you have to suffer like this? God is kind, Thatha, but fate is cruel." A sob escaped her, but she composed herself. She was not looking for sympathy, she was looking for meanings, and life was a hard taskmaster.

There was a pause, Thatha's arm pressing a little closer around his grandchild. "Dear Divya," he said, "the Law and the Lawmaker are not different. He has set the cosmos in motion in obedience to the Law, and we see His presence and manifestation in the workings of the Law. God and fate are not separable, Divya. The love of God is, forever and without exception, manifesting through his Law, and we see its workings as our fate. Fate or Karma is an integrated cosmic movement, one sweep of energy, but we fail to see that, and instead see the movement in personalized segments, lamenting over 'my fate'."

Divya smiled and ducked her head, a little embarrassed at her earlier outburst.

"Just as the sweep of causal energy is one unified flow over the whole of space, intertwining all lives, so is it also one flow over the whole expanse of time. There is neither beginning nor end, but one endless, seamless movement. You are not the physical form which is the gross body of matter; you are the psychic, subtle body that inhabits the gross body. The play of consciousness forms the subtle body, of which the scriptures say, 'Fire cannot burn it, nor waters wet it'. It is deathless.

"But the individual is not aware of his unceasing individuality and is afraid of death. He lives beyond death, but lives only to die again. The great yogi, Sri Aurobindo, has called this state as being 'immortal through renewed mortality'. This repetitive cycle of birth and death, to be reborn and to die again, is what is known to the wise as rebirth or reincarnation.

"Therefore, Divya, for you or for me, there was a past life before the one we are living now. It is not remembered, but forgetfulness does not negate what happened. The psychic link endures, and through it, the causal connectivity remains intact. Are you getting the point, Divya? You asked what you could have done in your young, unblemished life to earn the wrath of heaven and get this dreaded cancer.

"Here lies the answer, that it has to be the carry-over of residual causes from your own veiled past, coming to fruition in the ripeness of time, whose sequencing is beyond our deliberations. Do not say 'Divya has nothing to do with it', for Divya is not this body, it is the psychic person that is now Divya but was another before being born into this body as Divya."

"So I was someone else in my past life, Thatha?" Divya asked excitedly.

"Yes, my dear. But let us leave it there, with this understanding. Superficial scientific analysts or 'rationalists' may declare in their conceit that the idea of reincarnation is a primitive belief. It is not a random or baseless 'belief', though – it is based on the right interpretation of what everybody has, namely, consciousness. It is the science of life. Karma or fate or the law of causation, like the laws of material science, such as those of gravity or radiation, can never be in error.

I will say this again to you, my child, because this being understood, the futile question of 'why me?' shall never arise: There can be no effect without a cause, and cause and effect, like fire and heat, must be one in essence. As the cause, so the effect. No cause, no effect. A Sufi saint said:

> A thunderbolt would never strike a house, except that house drew it to itself. The house is as much to account for its ruin as the bolt. A bull would never gore a man, except that man invite the bull to gore him. And verily that man is more to answer for his blood than is the bull. The murdered whets the dagger of the murderer, and both deliver the fatal thrust.

"It is easy for men, particularly those of Western persuasion, to call this attitude fatalism and a supine surrender, but how can they, at a superficial glance, understand this language of a cosmic context? But you, Divya, have in you the seeds of knowledge that can germinate on this nourishment. Causation is never random, favourable or prejudiced, malevolent or benevolent. Leave Karma to its workings: whatever is… has to be, and what is not… could not have been.

"The pristine purpose of life lies beyond all this, beyond one birth or many births; these are all the workings of consciousness as mind. The purpose is to return to the source, the state of Pure Consciousness which is self-awareness. In that state, God and the I-person, or the ego-person, are one, even as a subject and its shadow are one. *Aham Brahmāsmi'* is this declaration."

※

18

Niranjan had been downcast and dejected while Divya had been in the hospital, but now he had returned close to his upbeat demeanour. Yet he was deliberately restrained, realizing what the family had had to pass through – the ordeal was stayed for the time being, but not wholly suspended yet.

"Mom," he said one day, "I had hoped that around this time I could ask Daddy if he would get me a second-hand motorcycle, but I've dropped the thought now. It would be selfish under the circumstances. I will concentrate on my approaching exams instead and I will surely score high. Then I will prepare single-mindedly for the entrance tests and earn my seat on merit. I know this is essential, for we have had to spend all we have on Divya's treatment, right, Mom?"

Raman, who heard it too, silently wondered whether there was not an undercurrent of subdued self-pity in the boy's mind. Would it amount to a trace of resentment too? How involved the human mind is, he thought, with its desires, its unending cravings and its limited means! Unknown to themselves, men live in the caverns of their subconscious, with eyes closed because they dare not see the naked truth. They are by turns jealous and angry and greedy, and show all the facets of selfishness, and they call this love. So it remains the only love in their relationships wherein everything is a bargaining, a tally of giving to receive in equal or larger measure, a transaction rooted in relativity.

In truth, love is the inherent nature of oneself, of one's own self, and the natural expression of one's being should be its self-contained fulfilment, as of the sun spreading its beneficial rays over the world, or of the flower wafting its delightful fragrance over the breeze, or of the breeze itself flowing across the hinterland in the ecstasy of its freedom: all natural and spontaneous indulgences of inherent *svabhāva*, asking for nothing, seeking nothing, needing nothing. Such is the inheritance of the human mind derived from divinity.

But all that is mostly forgotten, forsaken. Man imagines he is giving of his generosity to man and has a legitimate claim to the recipient's gratitude, and when he gives to the weaker or to the deprived, he believes he is sacrificing his comfort to give solace to another. In this, he deludes himself. The wise ones have said that sacrifice is charity done by a bankrupt on unsuccessful borrowing!

To start with, there is a bankrupt person. He should be struggling for survival, but he has a grandiose daydream of giving alms in charity. What does he have to give? He decides it can be done; all he needs to do is to borrow large amounts. But who will give a loan to a bankrupt? He will perforce be unsuccessful in his attempts at borrowing. Yet he considers he will do the charities, because he wants to feel the delight and dignity of having foregone the luxury of self-indulgence to transfer such luxury to another and call it sacrifice. Is it not all madness, all self-delusion?

Man is seeking enduring happiness all his life because his nature is derived from the divine which is the source of all life. The source is *Sat-Chit-Ānanda,* Existence-Knowledge-Bliss, and therefore man's nature must perforce be constituted of the same elemental qualities. Only in God do they exist in full measure, and therefore, in Him, there can be no void to be filled, whereas in the individualized form of a person, they are fragmented, incomplete and limited.

The limited man has his ephemeral existence within the large canvas of endless time, his little knowledge within the limitless expanse of true Knowledge, his wave of happiness based on relationships and possessions though surrounded by an ocean of unconditional bliss. Thus, incomplete, he longs instinctively for wholeness, but missing the truth of the way by which alone he can return homewards, he keeps on searching for it in the external world. Caught in the warp of time, he dies incomplete.

All his acts are to endorse his personal happiness; all his reaching out in love is only because of his love for his own self. Where then is sacrifice? And where indeed is the capital to invest outside oneself? And where the possibility of nature, since the natural has deviated into the unnatural?

This is the significance of the bankrupt's unsuccessful borrowing. This is the story of the perennial deception of our mind. Love is the truest name of the law of God. No love is possible except the love of self; the personal self, in reality, is not other than the all-embracing Self, which is God. God is all-love because He loves Himself.

And we are that too really. Love is not a virtue, love is a necessity. Seek no rewards for love; love is sufficient reward for love, as hate is sufficient punishment for hate. There can be no giving of love that is not at once an equal receiving; therefore, the fullness of love can never be reduced.

This is the divine truth that shines in a mind that is not deceived by the fallacy of time and space, and thus, not subjugated by causation. This is the freedom for which man is born.

Divya must understand this, then her trials and tribulations will be a peripheral aberration.

Raman was drifting deeper into his reverie. His own family today was the mirror in which he was seeing this spiritual history of mankind reflected. And he was seeing it not with any criticism or disapproval, but as a witness of creation. He was not a victim, but an observer standing apart, even from himself, so that he could see himself too as he saw all the others, and have the clear vision of the cosmic act.

Govinda tells me, recollected Raman, that twenty lakhs have been spent so far. Regular check-ups and the continued usage of very costly drugs will remain a regular drain of funds, which may go on for a year. There is no guarantee that leukaemia will not recur, and in that event, there is no escape from bone marrow transplant, which by itself may cost up to twenty-five lakhs.

By today's standards, we are at best an upper-middle-class family, and this is our plight. We would be stripped of all that we have and be heavily in debt. We may survive from hand to mouth, but where will it leave the children and all the dreams the family had for their education and glorious careers?

Like Govinda, his brothers are also good human beings, moral and ethical, and they have values that make up a united family, a harmonious society. They have already spent two and a half lakhs each for Divya, which is commendable, Raman thought. It is natural that they would be feeling that they have to support the cause further, unless Divya recovers from this stage and has no relapse. But at what cost to the needs of their own family can they support or should they support? There are no fixed answers to the question.

Yet the offers will come when the need arises. It will be a

sacrifice, for all their visual resources are already short of the envisaged demands. If they were to take loans for two or three lakhs each, it would mean lowering the bar for their own children's higher education.

Would it be right on Govinda's part to accept such offerings? If their love is seen in the giving, how can Govinda's love in the taking be evaluated? What is sacrifice in this, and what is selfishness?

Oh God, who can understand Your workings, and who can claim to be obeying Your Will, when one's own will, decision, and action form one's experiential reality, and God's Will can only be one's conjecture?

These questions can only be resolved in a mind that has crossed two barriers of ignorance; firstly, gaining the conviction that 'I am not the body, which is only a conglomerate of inert elements'; secondly, achieving the realization that 'I am pure Consciousness, unlimited and unconditioned, the energy of life in all beings, one and undivided'.

That known, there is no I-person to arrogate a will to itself, and deprived of will, there is no doership that can be claimed by the person. Action continues to be performed, but he who had earlier deemed himself the doer of the action is now seen as a device, an instrument of action. The will, the energy, the doership, all are arrogated by one self-conscious centre, the God of all creation.

Raman saw these truths vividly. He had a role in guiding the family, but that did not mean that he should pontify to them on matters that had personal implications for them, matters which could only be resolved by the individuals themselves, according to their leanings, capabilities and judgements. He would let his adult sons make their own decisions and follow their own counsels.

Spiritual truths can speak only to those that have an inward-focused mind and the ability to introspect with candour.

Otherwise, the truth will appear to be the false logic of self-justification, escapism or convenience. He cared for all the family in equal measure, but it was only Divya who showed promise of achieving redemption. Would she be granted time to fulfil that promise, or would she be plucked untimely?

Even so, God's care never abandons a sincere seeker, and the merit acquired is preserved and carried over in the continuity of the spirit, unhindered by the death of the body.

❦

19

Raman realized that if Divya was to be mentally prepared to meet stoically all the contingencies that now seemed within the realm of possibility, he should not, out of a misguided notion of sensitivity, shield her from the contemplation of death, as though it were a forbidden word.

On the contrary, he should encourage in her a detached and honest contemplation of death as a natural corollary to life, the two being the two sides of the same coin.

From study, contemplation and meditation over decades, Raman knew, beyond a shadow of doubt, that death was never born, and life never died! How mistaken is humanity with its tragi-comic conviction that there is an effect called death – when the very notion of death is inadmissible! – and that consequently life has to end in death – while life must laugh at the very concept of death!

This is not easily understood by all, and Raman knew that too. He remembered from his repeated readings of the great scripture of Bhagavad Gita that even Arjuna is originally confused on this point.

He therefore asks Krishna, the Lord Himself who was serving

as his mentor: "O Krishna, if I surrender my will and my action, opting instead to pursue the oneness of yoga with the Godhead, and without achieving that oneness I die, will I not be the loser on both counts?"

Krishna is forthright in His reply. "O Arjuna," says the Lord, "neither in this world, nor in the world to be, does such a person come to ruin. The one who has not fulfilled himself in yoga, though trying earnestly, will be reborn in circumstances propitious for the progress of the yoga. Such a one will regain the memories and skills acquired in the past and will diligently progress from where he left off."

So Divya must be established in these higher truths, Raman resolved. Though young in years, she has been blessed with a mind that can absorb such subtle revelations, and what is more, her heart and soul long eagerly to be led along these paths of thought. She should not allow her lofty ambition of self-realization to be diluted or diminished by the apprehension of impending death, however overwhelming such a probability may seem to one who has virtually a whole lifetime to anticipate.

Morning, noon, and evening, and often at bedtime too, Divya and Ramana Thatha conversed, and over several days, he told her, not too slowly and not too fast, about life and death, about pain and forbearance, about the predictable and the totally unexpected, about the mind's predilections and its absorption in the divine.

She heard with wonder and joy, felt space shrink and time stand still, and her whole being thrilled to the potential of the human to be one with the divine. Through many physical ordeals that she had to endure day after day, she strove to retain a sense of detachment from her body and to stay focussed, self-aware of consciousness itself, as apart from being conscious of things and events.

It was a goal worthy of saints and yogins, and here was a truly courageous girl yearning to achieve it. The angels must be applauding, thought Raman.

Around this time, there was good news for the family. Govinda's company chairman came on the phone personally and said, "Govinda, I am happy to inform you that the board of directors of our company has confirmed your promotion to the post of manager of factory operations. You will take charge at the end of this month. Congratulations."

"Thank you, sir," said Govinda. "I am grateful to the board."

"I expect Divya is better and will soon be normal. You may count on our support."

The spirits of all the members of the family were buoyed up and some relaxation soothed their tired minds. Divya asked, "Daddy, does it mean you will have more free time to share with us, or does it mean you will have even more work at the factory? Won't you come back a little earlier in the evenings and keep the weekends totally for us?"

The father replied, "It won't be any different, children, neither better nor worse. Life cannot be wished away, and, as they say in business circles, there are no free lunches! We have to work to earn, we have to strive to succeed, and in times of fierce competition, we have to keep running to stay where we are, or else, we will be carried backwards.

"I will create for myself a judicious mix of factory and family time. I will give of myself sufficiently to you."

"Our sweet Daddy," said Niranjan and Divya in unison, wrapping their arms around him.

That Sunday, the extended family got together, and it was a good deal like old times, except that Divya was more subdued and restful. For the adults, however, there was an undeniable undercurrent of anxiety. Being together was in itself an endorsement of sharing and caring, needing no more than a touch, a word, a smile.

When the children segregated themselves to hold their own counsels, one of them said, "Divya, my friend told me that, in their family, a boy was going through the same health problem as you, and that with the transplant, it would cost them one crore rupees."

Someone else asked, "What is a crore?" Came a reply: "Ten million." "Ten one-lakh notes will make a million?" "There are no one-lakh notes, silly!" "Why are there no one-lakh notes?" Divya, who had been silently listening, giggled. "Because the note would have to be the size of a plantain leaf!" she said. And now that wisdom had dawned all around, the question drifted away and some other subject sailed in.

The elders dared not probe the future, afraid of what shadowy forms may reveal their outlines and preferring to stay silent with comforting hopes. But they knew that the rough projections of medical probabilities would indicate further expenditure of about thirty lakhs.

They talked in general terms of the conditions prevailing in the country: of the crushing burden of ill-health and inadequate care, of abject misery and callous neglect, of brave talk of the government's involvement in the problems of the millions recognized as living below the poverty line of sustenance – B.P.L., which was a part of our vocabulary, in everyday use everywhere, but not a part of our soul-searching!

They spoke of statistics and grand statements made by politicians in public oratory, while everyone knew that billions of rupees were swallowed in corruption till barely one-tenth of the assigned amounts reached the targeted humans, and even that was given with no kindness, no sympathy, what to talk of love.

If privileged members of the middle class like them could not cope economically with the monetary demands of one case of cancer, oh God, how were the common people living their lives, when, along with cancer, heart problems, kidney failures, liver transplants, and uterus removals, stomach ulcers and brain haemorrhages and the like were prowling around menacingly, and when people were doomed to die before even expert diagnosis was possible?

But it helped nothing to dwell on it, except to know that crowds shared the level of misery they shared. For what purpose? Would a hundred deaths make one death less total, less intense, less agonizing?

Govinda spoke openly about the situation. "Thirty lakhs is a realistic estimate, if the problem recurs, and it might. I have thought it over carefully. I feel I can face up to the eventuality. You know that this property of my house is four 'grounds' in extent. When I acquired it, there were only a few scattered homes here, with wide open spaces in between.

"Since then, this area has become a favoured location for corporate executives and rising stars of the film world, and so the values here have gone up steeply and several good homes have been built. I built my house in two grounds and intended that a house may be built for Divya in the other half of the plot when I could afford it.

"Well, as they say, the carefully laid plans of mice and men are blown away like straws in the winds of destiny. Now I may have to sell those two grounds to raise some funds. So be it. I can look to my company's chairman for support on the security of my home.

"Up to the extent now envisaged, I feel I can manage. Let us not speculate beyond that. We are a strongly knit family.

"Ravi and Sekhar, you both have already helped me substantially. You need to consolidate your own future now. Let us leave it at that and see how the times ahead unfold."

❦

20

A few days later, Shastrigal and the astrologer, who were close enough with the whole family to take the liberties that familiarity permits, talked with the three brothers and fixed up with them that on the ensuing Sunday they would all meet at Govinda's house. It was imperative that urgent attention should be bestowed upon the zodiac in Divya's horoscope, and the requisite *homams* and pilgrimages be programmed.

Shastrigal and the astrologer were pleased with themselves that they had persuaded Govinda and Geeta to perform the *navagraha homam* and to undertake a pilgrimage. These events had produced visible effects in a short time and Divya's condition had improved miraculously, bearing testimony to the efficacy of their intervention, and validating the claims they made for their arts and skills. Now their further exhortations on the same lines could not but be accepted on faith, they felt, and it would be prudent to strike while the iron was hot.

So, on that Sunday, they were all together at ten in the morning at Govinda's home, the three brothers and their wives, with elderly Raman as an alert, yet detached, spectator. And though her presence went mostly unnoticed, Divya squeezed herself in and bid her time unobtrusively, acting as though her only purpose was to doze by her Thatha's side, while her true intent was to listen to what her Thatha may have to say.

The astrologer, having pride of place in this congregation, spoke first, thanking the gods who had heeded their prayers and, accepting their humble offerings, had responded with blessings which had checked and averted the malign influences upon the child's life at the moment and restored her to near-normalcy.

"But the planets keep their eternal vigil over the destinies of mortals, and as the planets run their ordained courses, our lives are made or marred, and our destinies moulded according to the laws enumerated in *Jyotishaśāstra*. To read the portents and administer the prescribed remedies is the duty we owe to ourselves and to our progeny; or else, we must blame not the stars but our own negligence.

"Divya's ascendant is Kataka, called 'Cancer' in the West. In her horoscope, the sixth house from the ascendant that she was born into is indicative of *ṛṇa* (debt), *roga* (disease) and *kalaha* (altercations) in her life. Śani (Saturn) is now in the sixth house. Not only is Śani the owner of one of the Maraka houses which are known to be killer houses, but it also so happens that Kethu is keeping Śani company now, and Kethu is a malignant planet whose combination with Saturn raises fatal possibilities.

"For Divya, this Śani *dasa*, which is in conjunction with Kethu, has been running for the past two years, and this is the reason for her body being afflicted with cancer. Kataka *rāśi* is in ascendance, and therefore Saturn is having a strong malefic effect on this horoscope.

"Śani can be controlled and subdued by Lord Siva, and therefore Govinda and Geeta should perform the sacred offering of circumambulating Arunachala Hill in Tiruvannamalai on the night of the full moon, after which, Siva pooja should be done, with *abhishekam* to Sri Annamalaiyar in the big temple. Shastrigal will make the arrangements with the temple priests.

"Sometime soon thereafter, on an auspicious day to be identified, the three ladies, if they so wish, considering the merit that will accrue to the three families, may worship the Lord at Kalahasti and perform a special pooja for Rahu and Kethu there. At home, they should light lamps each Saturday in worship of Saneeshwara, and distribute preparations made with gingelly seeds to a large number of mendicants, along with clothes for the *sādhus*. After completing these *sevas*, Mrithyunjaya *homam* must be done at home, with a prescribed number of priests chanting the *mantra* one lakh times along with performing certain oblations.

"Having thus invoked the blessings through *mantra* and *tantra,* the efficacy of *maṇi* must be harnessed. Specific precious stones bestow specific benefits and, rightly used, they are very powerful." The astrologer went on to say, "By a stroke of great good fortune, only a few months back, my elderly relative, a revered astrologer, decided to wind up his professional service, and offered me his rare collection of various precious stones. As the price was reasonable, and the acquisition a god-sent opportunity, I picked up the entire lot, knowing that he, with his expertise, had already ensured they were all flawless and of superior quality. A flawed stone becomes valueless as a talisman. So I can suggest and also offer to you the *manis* which Divya and Govida and Geeta should use. Surely there are indications that divine grace is awaiting us, if we follow the path shown to us."

A silence settled like fog upon the gathering, heavy with what had been said, and what besides might have been said, but was conveyed unsaid. Slowly, the women made their voices heard, a pathetic blend of distress and despair, dominated by an anxious urgency to act upon every proposal, for who knew where salvation lay, where grace was gained or where lost, and how could they afford a lapse or a mistake? It was not wealth or position or prestige that was at stake, but a precious life, and they must do anything and everything to safeguard it.

The three men murmured and muttered, strangers to their own minds, caught in a cruel conflict between emotional compliance and contrary compulsions. Divya kept her quiet stance, mostly unobserved, listening all the time and conscious of the grave problem of which she was the unwitting centre. She sensed the threads of religion and medicine, spirituality and science, even life and death, the imminent and the nameless future, all woven round her like the strands of a cobweb. And the brutal truth visible to her sensitive and sensible mind was that the saving of one member could demand the sinking of a family. But her Thatha had not spoken yet, so she waited.

❦

21

Raman was thinking to himself: Truth lies beyond the duality of life and death, even of God and devotee. All the dimensions of life, all the desires and delights and disasters are condensed into and contained in the reality of one's own being. The totality of the divine within the mortal being can be summed up in 'I am'. This being known, the whole of time and space and causation subside into Absolute Existence, which is manifested as the personalized ego-sense of the individual psyche.

The person misunderstands himself as the body he inhabits, and its protection, welfare and gratification become the goal and endeavour of a lifetime. In happiness and success, he forgets God; in sorrow and failure, he takes recourse to prayer and pilgrimage and ritual, and feels entitled to protection and prosperity all at once. God is summoned in our hour of need, not loved for His eternal benevolence. God's inviolable law of righteousness ensures that we get only the rewards we merit. It is not God, but our own faults that punish us.

Recognizing this error of perception and value and correcting it is the first step in cleansing our minds and clearing the mists of egoism that dim our vision of God; but it takes time to achieve the kind of clear vision that can burn away all our years of ignorance, and our despair cannot wait. Is it God that dallies in rushing to our rescue, or is it we who in our conceit believe that we can lightly bear all the burdens of life unaided, till the day comes when we find that we are being crushed by the load? Yet it would be adding insult to injury to accuse misguided humanity of its own perfidy in its hour of crisis. Compromise, not a rigid correctness, was the call of the hour.

Thus, making peace with the troubled moment when stating the harsh truth would only hurt and coated half-truths would hide but not heal, Raman spoke what he had to: "Our honoured guests of today," he said, conscious of the fact that Divya was listening alertly all the while, "have rightly guided us on how to unveil our destiny through astrological calculations and invoke the blessings of the deities through ritual and prayer, to annul all evil portents. God is the total cosmic authority and energy. Just as we expect God to respond to our call with love and grace, we too owe it to the Divine to relate to him with love and surrender. As we sow, so we reap. We must honestly admit to ourselves how far we can expect to be rewarded by the Divine for the hasty offering we now proffer; it will help us to keep our expectations on an even keel.

"There are more fundamental considerations. If the body is seen as the person, he or she is resolved into matter. Then all actions and interactions are in the realm of the physical; therefore, chemicals become the means for bringing about changes and cures. Flesh is acted upon by chemicals, medicines are administered to the body and we hope the toxic chemicals in the system will be neutralized and eliminated by the medicinal counterparts. When disease is chemistry, the saviour has to be chemistry.

But when we talk of prayer, we are talking of mind, not of matter. The interaction is between the consciousness of the devotee and the Total Consciousness which is God. If matter can relate to and react with matter, where is any doubt that mental consciousness can communicate with divine consciousness? God is the source of all activity and change; the minds of all involved, including the patient and the priest and the doctor, are the means through which change is wrought. Whatever happens has its origin and sequence in God. There is order, harmony, and justice in the law of causation that determines all events. This law is called Karma. It is never arbitrary, being always precise and consistent. The act of prayer and the result of prayer are part of the natural sequences of the causal flow.

"Each mind is the sum total of its own past carried as memory and shaped as desires. Thus, desiring happiness from the world outside through relationships, reactions, and possessions, each life runs its course. There is no finality to this quest for prosperity because new desires spring afresh and there can be no end to the process. Thus, we live a lifetime of trial and struggle, and die unfulfilled. The residual desires, as *vasanas*, constitute the subtle body, or psyche, that departs from the body at death. It has no option but to reincarnate. The quest for abiding happiness continues but never has an end, on this path.

"It can end, it must end, and that path is the path of salvation. Through surrendering the ego-sense to the truth of Total Consciousness, the partitioned and limited mind merges in the might and majesty of Absolute Consciousness. Only then can this temporal travesty of truth – relativity – end in the identity of the *jīvātmā* or the individual soul with the *Paramātmā* or God, like the stream merging in the ocean. This alone is to be wished for, longed for, worked for, and prayed for, till work and worship end.

"But the habituated mind resists because it has a vested interest in maintaining its 'individuality'. We pray for longevity, health and wealth as ends in themselves, and spare no thought for liberation or *moksha*. The bait of worldly pleasures in this life and heavenly ones after, in *svarga*, is too alluring. The eradication of individuality presents itself as void and terrifies. Thus is the mind deceived. This is what the scriptures have called *māyā*.

"We become victims of our own language. We say God is Immutable, All-powerful and All-knowing, and then mentally we structure a Being, an Existence, apart from the created beings, something or someone vast and mighty, and say, 'He created me. I am a puny creature born of His will, to be buried when He wills'. It is not so. He is the Creator and the creation, all of it at once, so that even now we are in Him, we are forever inseparably included in the totality. God, being changeless, has no need of time, for time is the medium of change. Cosmic creation cannot be without time, for it is ever-changing and shifting. This creation is made of mind and matter, and is therefore influenced by time-wrought changes.

"Astrology lays claim to be ranked as a science because it investigates the influence of time in cosmic phenomena. We call it *Jyotisha*, the science of light, because it throws light upon the unseen recesses of the future. What changes will occur with the passage of time are foretold from calculations based on mathematical coordinates. Scientists also need time and space as coordinates to measure velocity and acceleration when material forces like gravity act on matter, but those scientists do not include mind in their studies. The conclusions of astrology are not to be treated lightly. That is accepted.

"But the more pertinent question becomes: Do the stars actually affect human lives, or do they merely afford an index of events shaped by forces to which stars and men are equally subjected? Stars and planets are but manifestations of matter in space. The gravitational forces of these mighty masses act on each other. Matter attracts matter, and the force of attraction depends upon the masses and the distances separating them. All of creation, ranging from the grossest rock to the subtlest mind, is of this order, and nothing in creation escapes the gravitational pull. Let us concern ourselves today with what it does to our mind, because as we think, so we act; as we act, so we become. Our mind makes or mars our lives.

"While the laws of gravity apply equally to matter and mind, it must be noted that matter has no volition of its own, no awareness and no will, and therefore no conscious response to the forces acting on it; whereas the mind has a will, a determining capability and can add a force of its will to alter its course. This ability is clearly recognized as the *purushārtha,* with which the living person meets the impact of *prārabdha* karma and shapes its outcome.

"Now, astrology can locate the stars and planets in space at any given point of time, and chart the forces flowing from them to our earth, and the resultant vector of force felt on earth. The phenomena of elemental activities on earth consequent upon this prevalent force are deterministic and can be predicted accurately. Let the earth gyrate, let the tides ebb and flow, let the wild winds blow as determined. They are all insentient.

"But the results of this force on the mental phenomena of sentient beings can only be stated in probabilistic terms. The known mental disposition of the person is taken as the basis, and its known path of travel is extrapolated. To that trajectory is added the force of planetary influence at that time and the altered arrow of movement is calculated. This becomes the prediction. But this does not provide for the ability of the mind to change course by its own persuasions. If that happens, the prediction loses its validity.

"The influences of planets on man are classified under three headings, physical environment, mental peculiarities, and spiritual aspirations. I am speaking of those, and to those, who have the inner inspiration to live the lives of spiritual aspirants. To see clearly the luminescence of the divine, the glass chimney placed over that flame must be free from the smoke and soot of mental distortions. A coated chimney cannot be transparent and the light emerging through it can only be dim and hazy. Such a mind must be wiped clean and polished by the acts of prayer and ritual till the inherent lustre of the divine flame is restored. This is *chitta-śuddhi*, purification of the mind. It is activity or karma to be performed as per the vedic injunctions. It is a process that needs time to bear fruit.

"But if the mind has been purified earlier, not in expectation of fulfilment of desires, but as a natural flow of love towards God, of such a one, the scriptures declare that he has crossed the need to be selective and can simply be spontaneous and simple. A man of such purity of mind can say in his egolessness:

Yat yat karma karoti, tat tat akhilam
Śambho ta va āradhanam

(Whichever karmas are performed by me, all those karmas, oh Lord Siva, may they become worship of Thee.)"

Raman stopped talking. Immediately, he felt Divya quietly press her head closer against his shoulder. He bent his head imperceptibly nearer to her. He heard her whisper so only he could hear, *"Shambo ta va aaradhanam."* He knew then he had not spoken in vain – Divya had heard, Divya had understood, Divya was aspiring. Raman was content.

He had a few more words to say, and he spoke again. "I have

told you what I thought needs to be told. But it is not proper for me to tell any of you how you should decide now. We are in a crisis where decisions are not easily made. Money is a constraint and could become more so. We have committed ourselves to the medical treatment of chemotherapy and cannot ignore further attention from this team of doctors. There will soon be advice and pressure from friends to resort to alternative medicines, and decisions will have to be taken. Time management is also a complex factor here, involving the juggling of sessions in hospitals, office and factory, temples and pilgrimages. Discover your priorities and act with confidence in your judgements and with faith in God."

22

Divya returned to her school and there was festive cheer amongst her classmates and her teachers too, all of them genuinely delighted to have her back amidst them. Divya had thinned noticeably, even alarmingly. Her erstwhile cherubic cheeks were now sallow; her glowing skin had become pale; dark spots and patches were visible on her arms and neck; and, most distressing of all, her hair had dropped and thinned. She had had lovely tresses of dark, flowing hair with a silky gloss, but the side effects of chemotherapy, with its massive doses of strong chemicals, had predictably resulted in the shedding of her hair and the tainting of her complexion.

But Divya had earlier lived with unconscious ease with what nature had given to her, and now she seemed equally unconcerned about what nature chose to take back. Vanity and pride were alien to her mental disposition. Her eyes alone remained exactly as they had been, captivating pools of light and delight, spreading happiness innocently, like a flower its fragrance.

The school was readily willing to waive her lack of attendance in class and the missed lessons and tests, allowing her to continue her studies without any penalty. Her weakness notwithstanding, Divya made the effort to cope up with the handicaps, collected notes for the missed lessons, read up long portions that had been taught in her absence, and kept her goal set at the highest level.

But she found her grasp wavering, her memory weakened, and her comprehension somewhat laboured. Strive as she may, Divya, who had earlier been, easily and effortlessly, the brightest gem in her class, could not fetch a rank amidst the top ten now.

On one of those days, on returning from school, she sat near her Ramana Thatha in the seclusion of the western verandah of their house. There was peace in the air and mild warmth from the declining sun. "Thatha," she said, "my grades in school have dropped badly, but not from want of trying. My teachers and friends try to reassure me, saying that it is a passing phase, natural after the trauma I had to live through, and that I will soon return to my old scholastic levels.

"But that is not what I feel in myself – I've lost my motivation for worldly knowledge. I feel that the only goal my mind should aspire for now is the knowledge of knowledge – self-knowledge. In knowing oneself, all else is known. I am not protesting, Thatha. I am not even sad for myself, though I feel sorry that it will be a disappointment to my parents and my brother. I am only mentioning it to you."

Thatha replied, "I am glad you are not looking at it as a personal failure. Every event is one small current in a mighty cosmic flood. Events happen collectively; an individual cannot make them happen. A girl brighter than you could have joined your class, and then too you might not have earned the top rank. What real difference would that have made? You would still have been the same student that you had been.

"It is the mind dividing the event into separate individual components that creates a problem where none really exists.

When multiplicity is brought in, qualification and quantification become inescapable. The mind measures and counts; it weighs and values, and sets up conflicts and comparisons. Time and space are the concepts that distort and conceal the truth, break one into many, and set the parts one against the other. Fulfil yourself as you are, Divya, and be happy being yourself. Who knows what the future holds?

"Happiness is not determined quantitatively – it is not more and more of power or possession; it depends only on peace of mind. If you are not dependent on the external world for your happiness, what can mitigate your inner peace? You have had to bear your burden. And your academic potential has naturally declined. It may regain the losses in course of time.

"Meanwhile, put in your best efforts and be happy with the results. But be aware that nothing has happened that should reduce your love for God or faith in Him, and be content and comfortable in that relationship."

"Yes, Thatha," she said, "I do feel His love. And I am so fortunate, Thatha. I am surrounded by love – at home, at school, at the hospital. I could not have chosen this, much less made it happen. I can see the error that creeps in as personal doership and persists as egoism. You, Thatha, have been protecting me against this error which seems to be worse than cancer, and now that I am being tested, I will be on my guard."

"I am glad to hear you talk with such clarity of understanding. Ego is what each one of us has. It is the centre of all experience. It is the confirmation of consciousness in the person. Yet it is not what we take it to be. It is an image in the mirror and there is no substance in it. It is the shadow upon the ground, not the subject standing there. Its reality is its self-delusion. To know this is the fruit of self-enquiry, and to experience it as one's own truth is liberation or self-realization.

"As there can be no reflection without the subject to be reflected, there can be no false ego without the existence of the Reality that is God. God is Absolute Consciousness; man is reflected consciousness or the ego-person. I remember a small poem:

"Yesterday upon the stair

I met a man who was not there;

I met him again today.

I wish he would go away."

Divya clapped her hands in joy. "I get the point, Thatha, I get the point. How deluded one can be!"

The days passed, they always do. Divya's health had stabilized to some extent; the count of white blood corpuscles was still on the higher side but not alarmingly so; the platelet count was reassuring, and she was not running a temperature.

She had periodic medical check-ups when injections were invariably administered, for booster effect, for reinforcement, for immunity. The arms, riddled for so long with pricks that even a pincushion would have resented, had fortunately healed somewhat and she bore the ordeal quietly. She was trying to eat, without fuss or protest, such food as was appropriate for her nourishment, and her health was improving; there was even some weight gain.

All this was cause for relief to the family, but, to her doctors, it was not the light at the end of the tunnel. Cancer was such a wanton and wilful opponent of life that a trace of it left lingering in the body could bide its time, migrate unpredictably and emerge full-blown to be battled all over again. They wished their lovable patient had no malignant cells left in her system, but they could not presume anything and had to be prepared for a relapse.

If Divya fell ill again, bone marrow transplant would be an urgent necessity. Her parents and her brother would be the most likely candidates to donate marrow. So they were summoned to the hospital and tested for compatibility, but regretfully it turned out that none of them could be a donor for Divya. The hospital went through the system to locate other donors, but the chances were always slender and they had no positive response. They would have to source their requirements from USA or Europe where large banks of bone marrow were maintained.

A recent discovery in the treatment of leukaemia was the use of stem cells in lieu of marrow. Umbilical cord blood was used for the purpose. This material too was mostly not obtainable in India and had to be imported. To be prepared for any contingency, the hospital began tracking matching cord blood from abroad. The committed professional in Dr. Shankar never lost sight of his patient's possible requirements.

But even he worried over how the family would be able to meet the financial demands for importing such material. He knew the family was already in debt, and that a relapse needing a transplant would cost a king's ransom.

People easily blame the medical profession for the high prices, not knowing that the cost of the material inputs is itself so high. The real chance of a solution lay in the government's social policies but, in our country, where millions somehow survive below the poverty line, often not even having enough to eat, how can such health problems be resolved for more than a billion of its population?

❦

23

A few months passed by and the aching hearts slowly relaxed. At least outwardly, normalcy had returned to the household. Neighbours dropped in for light conversation, small shopping sessions for pleasure were not taboo, and friends of the kids came over on the weekends to play games. Laughter was no longer unthinkable; why, Divya was the one who often initiated the funny and the frivolous with a mischievous twinkle in her eyes. God was not forgotten by those who deemed Him the giver of grace in times of special need, or by those who knew the deeper truth that God and grace were synonyms, and grace was the only content in every act of God.

Geeta kept herself in touch with Shastrigal and the astrologer; frequently, special poojas were performed unobtrusively and appropriate gifts given. Who could define the anguish of a mother when her child lay exposed to the peril of death itself? Who could erase the fear that lurked in her heart, even though there was a smile on her face? Govinda went about his duties manfully, relieved that the threat of deluge had mercifully receded; his dear child was still his to hold. The awareness of his massive debt could not be erased – in honesty, should not be erased – till it was repaid. It stretched his resources to the full, but a kind fate had seen to it that it did not breach the bounds of possibility, and in five years his freedom would have been redeemed.

At the other end of the spectrum was Raman, who knew that God was the seamless truth of one's existence, never apart, though unrecognized due to man's ignorance. If He was the giver, He was also the taker; if He was the blessing, He was also the punishment; if He was pure love, He was also impartial justice. He was not merely to be prayed to, He was to be possessed.

Where does the individual ego go when tired of its vain wanderings in the thorny fields of sense perceptions, when it despairs of fulfilment and longs to return home? One may ask, where does the shadow go after its long trek in the sun? Where does the image go after residing in the mirror? Do not the shadow and the reflection merge with the subject, the only reality, which had caused the false shadow and the false image, while itself remaining unaffected and unaltered? So too, for the false and deluded ego, homecoming is a merger, not merely a meeting. Merger with what? With the truth. With reality. With God. With one's own actuality.

This is what I am living for, striving for, thought Raman to himself. And this is what I want to embed in Divya's heart and head. She is able to understand and imbibe it. Whatever her destiny, however long her lifespan, she can receive the message and the method and reach Home. I do not know what is in store for her, maybe years of good health, heights of achievement, career, marriage and family, and material prosperity. If so, let it be, but nothing in it should change her spiritual aspiration and attainment.

Our scriptures have said that the one who attained self-realization, the *sthita-prajña*, may be seen by the world as a beggar or as an emperor, as a child or as a madman, but in truth, regardless of how others saw him, he would be the Perfect One. If it should be Divya's lot to have a relapse of cancer, to go through intense pain and bodily agony, and to die at a tender age, then so be it, but even through such an ordeal, the acquired truth can sustain her spirit, and, casting off the body, she would be liberated, would have attained *moksha*.

As Raman was ruminating thus, Divya came and sat by his side. "What are you thinking of, Thatha?" she asked, half-knowing the answer by instinct.

Thatha replied: "Divya, the discovery of God is the discovery of oneself. 'Know thyself' is both the root and the tree of all knowledge. I was remembering what a saint had said: 'Oh God, for a long time I sought you and found myself. Now I seek myself and find you.' That is why I have been telling you that to know yourself, you should experience the higher truths of your own existence, namely, that you are not the body, you are not even the mind that knows the body but knows not its own source. Then you arrive at the transcendental truth that you are pure Awareness, the Absolute Consciousness. Divya, never stop dwelling on this great revelation and soon enough it will dawn on you as experienced reality.

"Divya, the relationship between a devotee and the Lord breaks all the bounds of human interaction. A saint, a *fakir* (mendicant), once sang:

Oh Lord,

What I, a mere beggar, desire of you

Is more than a thousand kings could wish.

Everyone has a request to make of you,

But I have come to ask you for yourself."

Divya's face was beaming. "How beautiful, Thatha. Yes, indeed, what else can compare with that gift?"

❧

24

Two blocks away from Ravi's house was located a church. Though the number of Christians amongst that predominantly Hindu population was not high, the church had been built quite lavishly, with wide open areas on all sides, and a pretty garden with a lawn in front and flowering shrubs all round. Two borewells assured copious supply of water, though the area had to face the problem of scarcity of municipal water for six months in the year.

Funds seemed to be no problem, though the small congregation was relatively less wealthy than the rest of the neighbourhood. Opulence seemed to smile on the inmates and even more on the hierarchy that ran the institution. Ravi had only a nodding acquaintance with the pastor of the church, a man his age, and seemingly well pleased with himself and his occupation.

It was a surprise to Ravi when, one Sunday afternoon, a car glided to his porch and the pastor, in his unmistakable attire, with a silver cross upon a chain dangling on his chest, stood at his doorstep, smiling disarmingly. "Greetings and welcome, Father," said Ravi. "Please step in. We are honoured by your visit." Ravi's wife had come out by then and, folding her hands together in salutation, said, "Please come in."

When they were seated in the living room, the pastor said, "Though our acquaintance is slight, your family is an asset to this community. I know that your brother Sekhar lives in this neighbourhood, while your eldest brother, Govinda, is also not far away. I learnt many months ago that Govinda's daughter, Divya, had had the misfortune to be afflicted by cancer and was hospitalized. This I came to know through contacts in the school where the child studies.

"I have heard that there has been a remission of her sickness and that she is back home now, but I can imagine how much anxiety and worry must persist in the family. I have come to you to express, through you, to the whole family much more than my sympathy, to speak of the love and care that Jesus has for Divya, and of His command to me and my congregation to pray for her total recovery and to stand by you and support you in every way we can. You are our brethren."

The lady went in to make tea. Ravi said, "You are very kind, sir. We deeply appreciate it." In his mind, he could not help thinking: This person is well informed about our family, almost as though we are targeted for the love and care he speaks of. Unless he was making enquiries and had informants, he could not know all that he now knows, because we are virtually strangers to him and we are rather orthodox Hindus.

Tea was served amidst trivial exchanges. As the visitor rose to leave, he said, quite casually, "It would be nice if you and your brothers stopped by the church some day for a while; we can pray together for a few minutes."

In due course and without any special emphasis, Ravi informed his brothers about the pastor's visit and conversation. The others let it pass, but it was a hook that caught in the bruised folds of Geeta's motherly heart, which, even in the absence of visual distress, could not cast away its anxiety. Any word of hope and any suggestion of divine favour compelled her distraught mind to cling to it and to build upon it.

A month later, the pastor met with Ravi again – whether by intent or by chance, it was not clear – and renewed his proposal that they attend the church once, merely as a token of good fellowship. This was cause enough for Geeta to persuade her husband to agree to the visit, till Govinda had to concede there could be no harm in doing so if it meant so much to her. He mentioned the situation to his father as it seemed to be the proper thing to do.

Raman appeared to be surprised by the news. He looked into Govinda's eyes and slowly said, "It is a small thing. Yet it is not a small thing either. I will speak my mind about it if and when the time comes for me to do so. For the present, I will leave it to the discretion of all of you as adult individuals. You have to listen to your hearts." He knew in the recesses of his mind that the church had an agenda, but to dwell on it now would be a lost cause. Let time brew the sinister concoction and then he will throw it into the dust.

When Geeta was told exactly what Raman had spoken, her troubled heart could only hear its own cry of desperation – Won't you protect my child? – addressed to everyone and to no one. Govinda consoled her and said he would do whatever pleased her in the matter.

Divya was getting better with the passing days and the prospect of complete recovery could be hopefully projected. The urgency for related activities had eased. Geeta too had relaxed a bit, but she could not set any less store now by the rituals and pilgrimages that her mind had earlier sought frantically; the proposals and persuasions of Shastrigal and the astrologer were constantly flowing into her ears. Already another *homam* had been performed at home, and two visits to temples in other towns undertaken. The costs involved were a glaring actuality that could not be ignored by Govinda, but it would be sacrilegious to talk of it to Geeta – seeing her state of mind, he bore it all silently and with sympathy.

At school, the regular routine continued, and, for Divya, it was like old times again. She loved her classes and the learning process; her rank had risen, though she was not as outstanding in her exam performances as earlier, but it did not affect her contentment any more.

Adolescent schoolchildren, just entering their teens, are innocent and uninhibited. Their forthright candour may even seem cruel, but it is not cruelty, it is still unblemished innocence. So Divya's classmates talked freely, without inhibition, what came into their tender heads. So sometimes one said: "Divya, we heard you were dying. Once, the buzz was that you had died. I even cried. But then our teacher said you were alive. Did you die for a while? How was it, Divya?"

"I did not die. I went briefly into coma."

"Were you afraid you would die, Divya?"

"I knew there is no death for the soul. I knew I am the soul."

"You talk like that because of your orthodox religious training. We all have to die, Divya."

"Yes, true, all our bodies will turn into corpses one day."

"Divya is mentally affected by her ordeal. Who wouldn't be? See, her grades also have gone down," they muttered amongst themselves.

"Maybe that is the truth, my dear friends."

"Did you have lots of pain?"

"Yes, the body was often racked with pain."

"Oops, the bell has rung. Let's go. Divya, sit next to me."

Another month passed. Divya's family informed the pastor of the church through Ravi that they would like to attend prayers next Sunday, and there was a warm response. Accordingly, the three men and their wives went to the church, and, despite being greeted by the pastor personally and by a few other prominent members, requested that they be allowed to sit unobtrusively amongst the crowd. During worship, they did what the others did, knelt when others knelt, and rose when they rose, and said "Amen" when they heard it said.

When the pastor spoke, apart from the sermon which told of the love of Jesus Christ for his flock, and of the only son of God who was given to mankind to be their only true Saviour, he changed the subject and said: "Faithful believers in Jesus who are gathered here today, we have in our midst a family that we have invited to join in our worship. We welcome them in the name of Jesus the Lord, and bring before Him for His mercy the distress they are facing. A daughter of this house, of tender years and great potential, has had an untimely visit from Satan in the form of cancer. After much suffering, she is relieved of it at the moment. You will all join me so that with our prayers to the merciful Father in Heaven through our saviour Jesus, we will ensure that the evil spirits dare not return to her vicinity.

"Our Father God has said that the keys to the Kingdom of Heaven are given to those who sincerely believe in Him. I plead with our guests of today that they may so believe in our Father. I declare in the mighty name of Jesus that their child's body will become His temple, and I command any sickness or disease that has been trying to attack her body to flee in the name of Jesus, so that this child of our community can present a healthy body to our Lord as a living sacrifice unto Him. In Jesus' holy name I pray, Amen."

When the ceremonies ended, Govinda, his brothers, and their wives waited on the sidelines till the pastor came up to them. "Thank you, sir, for praying for Divya," said Govinda, sounding low-key because the words spoken by the pastor had seemed sectarian, somehow coloured and motivated, though he could not define his unease with the moment. Geeta merely felt that God's help had been invoked and a great benefit had been reaped. The pastor gauged that the father was undecided and the mother willing; the camel would be invited into the tent. To him, it was a moment to savour.

25

Another eight months passed with relative calm. Divya had written her school examinations, not without distinction, and there were two years yet before her academic achievements would impact on her future prospects, so this was not the time for anyone to feel any concern about it.

Niranjan had also taken his final exams and done well. But in the choking pressure of prevailing academic competition, when receiving 98 percent marks spelt being rocketed into a sublime orbit, while getting 97 percent could mean the dashing and crashing of all ambitions, as though the one defined a genius and the other confirmed mere mortality, Niranjan could not be confident that he would clear the cut-off barrier for entry to most engineering courses. The family could not fault him as he had indeed brought to his studies all the diligence and industry he was capable of. The result was awaited.

At home, the efforts for divine appeasement and compassion, as guided and initiated by the ordained intermediaries, namely Shastrigal and the astrologer, had to run their course, on Geeta's request, for who could tell which omission would invite disaster and which acquiescence would fetch the reward? So there were periodic poojas and pilgrimages, the acquisition of nominated precious stones for each one at precious prices, and the gift of a gold ornament to the all-powerful Kali, the divine mother who gave life or took it away. A lakh-and-a-half had been thus added to the expenditure. It was a burden, but "What if...", "How else...", "For, can you not see, Divya has been well..." were among Geeta's refrains.

Divya was deep in thought on the same issues, involved intently in what was happening to her, personally, and to the family, collectively; but beyond both, she wanted to see and sense the operation of Karma or the cosmic law of causation, which was declared to be infallible, dispensing justice to all always. So she came on silent feet to her Thatha as he sat in the verandah, wrapped in quietness, laid her hands in his lap, and said "Thatha, I am troubled by a question."

"Ask me, child."

"Thatha, *homams* have been done for my welfare, *mantras* have been chanted, pilgrimages undertaken, alms given. I have recovered or am recovering. Is there a link, Thatha?"

"Every cause manifests its effect, Divya. That is the link. It cannot be in isolation that a specified cause links with a specified effect. Causation (Karma) is a flux. It is a total movement. The stars affect me, and as truly, I affect the stars. Our minds are limited and they ask questions of the unlimited. But there can be only tentative answers. The absolute truth is beyond questions and answers, being beyond the mind."

"Thatha, I have a suspicion you are bypassing my query to take me on the fast lane!"

"Clever girl! In a way, you are right. Karma is for the individual and there is no salvation till one goes beyond individuality. The disease is of the body, health is desired for the body, and the poojas are intended to support the body. We can discuss that, but do not ever forget that you are not the body, you are consciousness. In the Bhagavad Gita, Krishna tells Arjuna about the field, *kshetra*, and the knower of the field, *kshetrajña*. You are the knower of the body-mind entity called Divya. Now ask me, what is it you want to know?"

"Thatha, Divya became afflicted by cancer. Poojas and *homams* were performed according to scriptural injunctions by qualified priests. We may assume there were no lacunae in the execution. Is it not mandatory that Divya should be restored to normal health? In fact, Divya is well as of today. Is there an implication that she will continue to be so? Thatha, I do not ask from personal anxiety; I want to understand, in personal terms, the operation of the laws of Karma. I want to study the fate of Divya." She laughed and added, "I happen to know her quite well!"

Ramana Thatha joined in the laughter. He was happy at her extraordinary perceptiveness and grasp. He said, "The poojas have surely played their role and made their contribution. Remember it is Total Consciousness that directs the cosmic play of events. Our poojas and prayers are all recorded in Total Consciousness; nothing is missed. Everything is received and rightly responded to. All desires are heard, all factors are computed in totality, and what is deserved therein is the result, the effect. The law of causation functions automatically and is the serene justice of God. *Prakṛti* or Nature is the eternal manifestation of this 'natural' rightness. Concepts of accidents, luck and chance are our mental anomalies. How can something 'unnatural' happen to 'nature'?"

"Where does it leave me, Thatha? Am I not entitled to conclude that if I live on, the poojas have delivered on their promise, but if I die of cancer, the poojas were futile and powerless?"

"No, Divya, that would indeed be a gross misunderstanding

of the cosmic order. Almost invariably, our prayers are not born from a surrender to the will of the Almighty, which would mean a loving acceptance of causal connectivity and consequence. Our prayers are petitions that our personal will may be fulfilled, and that reflects our egocentric mentation. Our petitions are addressed to, and will reach, the ordained divinities that administer the various segments of the management of cosmic activity. These divinities are not the makers of law – that remains the sole will of the Lord; they are administrators of the law as it is laid down. Causal determinism binds them, just as it binds mortals. Every response has to be true to the holistic frame. No man is an island; what affects one also affects a continent.

"What is deserved rightly by Divya the person has been given to her, and by the same act, your whole family (including me), your doctors and a wide circle whose shores are lapped by the ripples from these events have been given what is rightly their due to enjoy or suffer. How can we say what that is or should be? We only know you are well now, for that is the right poise of events for today. How can we know what lies in store ahead?

"But again, why should we know? Why should Divya be concerned of the future when she has touched the immortal truth of Time itself: that 'time' as we know it is the misleading myth of our lives, that time is a mental concept and thus part of consciousness, whereas Divya is not this body but eternal Consciousness? Established in that truth, identified with the Absolute as indicated by the Vedic declaration *'Aham Brahmāsmi'* (I am Brahman or God), you can now see the illusory play of prayers and penance, rewards and retributions, health and sickness, life and death. Do you understand, Divya?"

"Yes, Thatha, I see the tapestry of life better now. You are pointing out to me that the scriptural injunctions and all the rituals of religion have the strengths and merits attributed to them and they are truly operational. But they naturally become one of the several factors that together define the outcome. The pulls and pushes of all the other factors will also contribute their dynamics to the final outcome. Being limited in our knowledge of the totality of causal forces, we cannot see the unerring justice of karmic operations. We live with our desires; we are not honest about what we deserve. Thatha, the lesson is simple – leave it to God."

Ramana Thatha closed his eyes, held Divya's hand lovingly, and fell silent. More words would only disturb the communion between Divya and God.

26

Yes, it is true that Divya had been well so far, but now a fever came upon her and, try as she did to play it down, it persisted the next day and the next. There was loss of appetite, and pallor on her face. Alarmingly, she had a nosebleed and also developed pinprick bleeds, a clear indication of deficiency in the clotting of blood. Anxious and perturbed, the elders hastened with Divya to Dr. Shankar.

While trying to maintain an appearance of calm appraisal, the doctor was by instinct deeply concerned. A routine check had been done at the hospital less than three months ago and every parameter seemed under control, but now it seemed that serious deficiencies had cropped up and increased rapidly. He ordered blood tests and other clinical tests and the results were studied the next day. Haemoglobin in the blood was at a low 7.5 gm/dl instead of the healthier minimum of 12, white blood corpuscle count was at an untenable 60,000, and platelet count was critically low, all suggestive of acute leukaemia.

Divya was admitted as in-patient and, by way of containment, she was treated with chemotherapeutic drugs, oral steroids and antibiotics. After that course of medication, she was placed under general anaesthesia and some marrow was aspirated from her hip bones for running further tests.

When all the test results came in, Dr. Shankar knew that his patient had a relapse of ALL, Acute Lymphoblastic Leukaemia, and her condition was life-threatening. Confirming this to the family was always the most painful, sensitive and difficult moment in his life, even though his professional speciality inflicted this compulsion upon him repeatedly. Sorrows do not become more acceptable with time, nor do they make it less oppressive to endure new ones. Each sorrow has a fresh start and brings a fresh pain in all its intensity. Yet sentiment had to wait when work beckoned.

The elderly Raman, in a pensive mood, Govinda, with his mind rushing into the future, and Geeta, numbed by an intuition of what might follow, sat with Dr. Shankar in his office. And the doctor began: "I am sorry, but I have to confirm that Divya has a relapse of blood cancer. The usual treatment is through bone marrow transplant, which unfortunately has to be ruled out in this case, because I have been at it for months already by way of precaution, but I've been unable to find a suitable donor. Autologous marrow transplant, where Divya's own marrow would be taken and, after a high-dose treatment, given back into her body when it would grow and fulfil her needs – sadly, this too has to be ruled out because Divya does not have marrow to spare that we can use.

"But we are not lost. Medical science has found a new source of blood-forming stem cells in Umbilical Cord Blood. This is blood that is left behind in the placenta and the umbilical cord after the delivery of a baby; cord blood is rich in stem cells and can be used instead of bone marrow for transplantation. Stem cells are blood cells at their earliest stage of development in the bone marrow, before they have become committed to developing into white cells (which fight infections), red cells (which carry oxygen), and platelets (which control bleeding). It is these 'mother' cells which are the key factors in transplantation.

"Here again, I have taken action to be prepared for just such adverse developments as we are facing. Cord blood is almost impossible to obtain in our country, and needs to be imported from USA or Europe. I put the system to work long ago, and some shortlisting has been done. Now we can pick up the links and get the matching cord blood in two or three weeks.

"Please come back after three days. I will have a single room made ready for Divya, to protect against any possibility of infection. Regular doses of drugs and some blood tests will be required. A tube known as a central tube may be inserted into her body under local anaesthesia to avoid numerous individual injections. A high dose of chemotherapy is necessary. There may also be a need for cranial radiotherapy, to prevent migration of cancerous cells to the brain and neural system.

"I am giving you some details so that you will appreciate that what follows will be intensive and involved treatment. She will feel better after it and I believe she can stay at home for some days while we await the arrival of the imported cord blood.

"All this inevitably implies huge expenditure. The imported material by itself will cost you around twelve lakh rupees. All the other inputs, some I have mentioned, and there are others, will cost another ten lakhs or more. You must prepare yourselves to meet the burden, we have no choice."

Silence for a long moment, indicating that the doctor had said it all.

"Yes, doctor. There is no choice. About twenty-five lakhs. There is no money. Yet there is no choice." That was Govinda's response.

A sob, choked by great effort – that was Geeta's.

Umbilical cord – every birth comes with one. And it is promptly thrown away, got rid of. It has given of itself to life already. But if needed again, if called upon to partake as another life support, twelve lakhs are needed. What a beggar woman would throw off in an unvisited corner of land finds a desperate seeker, and it costs twelve lakhs. Do we laugh or do we cry? Those were the thoughts that came to Raman. He did not speak them, he only thought them. What was the use of speaking?

Govinda fought manfully to recover his composure, for on him had fallen the responsibility to resolve the unprecedented dilemma they had to face. Without an assured backup of another twenty-five lakhs, he could not proceed, lest he should find himself drowning in midstream. The only strong support left to him was the prospect of mortgaging his house; other supports could only be nominal, such as more loans from his bank or what he could borrow from his brothers.

But every rupee would have to be repaid and he was already chest-deep – or was it neck-deep? – in debt. His mind wandered; Divya would recover and her future education would raise its monetary demands; and then her marriage would need a small fortune. And there was Niranjan. But he forced himself to return to ground realities and he thought no further than the finances for medical treatment. He would talk to his chairman.

Around this time, the pastor got in touch with Ravi and Sekhar. He had cultivated affinity through periodic contacts ever since their first meeting, and he always seemed updated on information regarding Divya, be it her schooling, her health, or her hospitalization. He even knew what treatment was being administered now or being proposed for the future, and the costs involved. It all seemed rather uncanny, unless it was assumed that he had vigilant informants both at the school and at the hospital. If so, it could not be just for one Divya, or one school, or one hospital. Collecting information about people in distress and in need in that area seemed to be the strategy. Could it be for love and compassion alone? The pastor would perhaps claim it as self-evident, yet somehow it was not convincing. But a half-blinded man on a desperate journey cannot wait for a clear view of his path forward; he must stumble along, accepting the consequences and pitfalls. Divya's family was in no position to engage in polemics.

The pastor was periodically meeting Ravi and Sekhar at their homes, together or individually, and prevailing upon their patient audience while he built up his discourse, the burden of which was: "At present, the state of Divya's health is serious and brooks no delay in efficient handling. The church, and I as its servant, are deeply distressed, yet we know that the merciful Father in Heaven will heed our prayers and set her on the path to recovery if we do things the right way in His name.

"You have, I agree, left her care in the hands of competent doctors, but that is not enough. Besides, the treatment has already consumed your financial resources, fairly well-to-do as you are, and you are not even halfway through the projected costs. The church is blessed with strengths in this area by the generous support of the faithful, and is eager to be of help. I feel within me the voice of Jesus telling me that Divya's life should be saved in His name. We need to undertake this together. The love is His, provided we match it with our faith, and you will have to prove your willingness before Him; the rest will be easy.

"You must arrange at the earliest that we all meet at Govinda's house, when I will reveal fully our course of action. I know that your father will be there, and that, as the head of the family, his blessings are essential for the proposals. In the given situation, I believe he will recognize the utility of what I say and will agree. Please lose no time. The Lord calls."

❦

27

Ravi and Sekhar called up Govinda and requested him to meet them at Sekhar's house the same evening. They narrated to him as closely and completely as they could all that the pastor had said to them. His words had implied that the church would extend monetary support, though this was not clearly spelt out. Obviously, there was a catch to it, but in their hour of desperation and frantic need, some compromise would be inevitable and there was no canon against even considering the proposals.

So Govinda sat with his father, Raman, and told him everything in sequence, not overlooking the previous meetings with the pastor and what had been spoken then. Raman listened silently, and the more he heard, the deeper the silence itself seemed to grow.

Finally he sighed and said, "I agree with the pastor's last words, the Lord is calling. He is calling upon the pastor to speak, and He is calling upon me to speak to him in reply. Meanwhile, do not be deluded into believing that easy remedies are awaiting us. Our lines of Karma will flow with causal correctness, as always. Providence maintains its functions as normally ordained; it is the mind of man that manoeuvres its means to suit its personal ends and selfishly creates disharmony. I will speak, more so because there are truths that my sons need to hear. Arrange for the pastor to visit us as early as it suits the three of you and the pastor."

That was done and the four met with Raman. There was a quiet air of austerity on the occasion and the greetings were subdued. The pastor had about him an air of confidence, if not of conquest. He said he was honoured to meet the head of the family, a family revered in the community and an asset to all of them. That a child of such a family should be in untimely distress was cause for the deepest grief and concern. As a humble servant of Lord Jesus, he knew, in the certainty of his faith, that a remedy was on hand and he had come only to enlist their responsible cooperation to achieve redemption for the child.

In their scriptures, the Lord has said that, through Jesus Christ, anyone who believed in Him and agreed to follow His guidance would be redeemed right now in the name of Jesus, and no sickness or disease formed against that one shall prosper any more. In His Word, He has promised that He will restore such a believer to health and heal all wounds. "My brothers in faith, this is what I wish to make possible for Divya. We should immediately place her under the best medical care that we have in the country, and fortunately such care is available in a Christian Mission hospital only two hours' drive away from our city. I can request our honourable bishop to contact the director of that hospital on your behalf, and her admission there can be organized urgently. You will kindly permit me to use the same channel to see that all costs of treatment are waived; in the church, there is provision for it."

The pastor paused in his narration at this significant point. Geeta had silently come in while the pastor was speaking and was standing behind the men. On hearing what she heard finally, her hands went up to her throat, and she stared, unbelieving, yet uplifted. It was not missed by the pastor, who was seated facing the men. In this game, which he was used to playing incessantly, one weak link often spelt victory.

The pastor picked up with deft fingers the threads of the net he was weaving adroitly: "I have even kept the church's ambulance vehicle ready to leave at a moment's notice, in case your hospital takes umbrage at shifting the patient and denies support. There is only one requirement from our side. You must allow me to baptize Divya. That is important. Once that is done, and the small matter of a Christian name for her is implemented, you can leave everything else to me.

"I implore all of you to get into the spirit of what I am initiating, but I will leave it to each one of you individually to surrender to Lord Jesus, with the conviction that He is the only Son of God, who was set upon our earth to save mankind from its sins and turn men back from worshipping false gods. He sacrificed His only son so that His blood may save us. But we can come to this in the days ahead; the only important thing now is protecting Divya. I plead with you as an emissary of my Lord to agree because, without this one factor of baptism, my hands are tied. Do not hesitate. Baptism is a form of rebirth, by water and the spirit, and rebirth for Divya is what we are looking for."

The pastor stopped talking. Geetha moved close to Govinda, and in a voice meant to be a whisper, but which, in her emotion-charged state, carried far enough to be overheard by all, she said, "What is he saying? What is baptism? Please tell me. I will do anything to save my child."

Govinda said gently, "The pastor wants Divya, now, and us, later, to become Christians. Baptism is how they make a Christian out of you. Then they will call Divya 'Diana' or 'Doris', or something like that. They will treat her free of cost in the best hospital. Please remain silent."

"I can't. How can I? Give me my child. You had said that another twenty lakhs are needed now. Have you got it?"

Govinda replied, "I hope to manage. I have not yet had the time to work it out."

"Why can't we agree with the man of the church? Between life and death… Oh, my God, do these things matter?"

The pastor was tactful. He smelt success, but he knew he should not betray his personal anxiety. "I think I should leave now, and, if you permit, return tomorrow. It will give you time to consult amongst yourselves and come to a decision, even though, let me add, the only right decision is self-evident." He rose to leave.

"Please sit down, sir." Raman had spoken in a firm voice that compelled compliance, and it took everyone by surprise. The pastor sat down.

Raman said, "I speak in sorrow, not in anger. I speak because of the pain I feel, and not because there is a call to retaliate. I do not claim to know your ancestry, but I can say, based on historical precedent, that within a measurable period of time, your forefathers were Hindus, worshiping the gods we now worship, and in the same way. Somewhere down the line, under pressure of circumstances, someone in your lineage broke ranks. If it amounted to a betrayal, it did not outweigh the hardships that were being endured, with no prospects of relief for ages to come – the hardship of hunger and privation, the survival amidst sickness and poverty, and the humility of social discrimination. They were real problems of life, and relief was unexpectedly forthcoming through Christianity.

"But it came at a cost. The hardships suffered by your forebears were not tortures of the soul; they were tortures of the stomach. But those that came as saviours demanded that you sell your soul for them to salvage your body. You were asked to forsake your ancient faith, and you said, it is done. They asked you to swear your faith in a replacement they proposed, and you said, done. Transactions in faith performed at command! If only you would leave God out of it, and truthfully say, 'I will pursue my chosen career of selling faith based on names and words, and secure my own material well-being', that would be honest. But your age-old modus operandi is: Feed the belly, bleed the soul; cure the body, lure the spirit. What deceit!

"Have you made the effort necessary to understand what concept that word 'God' implies? Have you gone into the heart of that thought? I have and I will tell you. There is no Hindu god and Muslim god and Christian god and Parsee god. All those to whom name and form and temporality are affixed are existences, real or mythical, to be revered and worshipped, as they lead the distracted mind towards peace, the evil mind towards virtue, the sorrowing mind towards solace, the limited mind towards perfection.

"All these are happenings in consciousness, and you and I and all others possess consciousness. That is the energy of life; that indeed *is* life. Though experienced as individual minds, consciousness cannot be partitioned, any more than space can really be broken into independent bits of space. Therefore, there can only be Total Consciousness, which would automatically be All-knowing – for how can there be any existence not known to knowledge? Then Omniscience or All-existence (Omnipresence) would also apply to Total Consciousness. This Total, Supreme, Absolute Consciousness is equated to God.

"Since we are all conscious beings, not one of us is distanced from or disowned by the Godhead. We belong together, which makes God all-inclusive. At the same time, since the whole is greater than the sum of its parts, God is transcendental and surpasses all our qualitative and quantitative measures and our spatio-temporal concepts. We remain the effects of a functioning consciousness, while He abides as Pure Awareness. We exist in relativity, whereas He remains Absolute. The relative cannot stand apart as the relative and imagine that it can experience the Absolute, but it can merge into the Absolute and then know that indeed it had never been discarded by God nor ever separated from Him, in truth. 'I and my Father are one,' said Christ and this is what he meant, but which amongst you that speak platitudes from the pulpit has understood it? That is my sadness for your sake.

"One of your own celebrated philosophers, some centuries back, said in personal grief and public sarcasm: 'The last Christian died upon the cross.' Need I explain what he meant? That Christ was not understood by those who took his name in vain, that Christ's exhortations were never implemented, and that what he symbolized died with him.

"Yet, God be praised, the ancient truth that he revisited is not lost for humanity. It is there in the Hindu Vedanta from times immemorial, it is there in Sufi teachings, and in Zen sayings. It is also there in Christian mysticism.

"But the church does not want to recognise the fact, because the church has adhered too adamantly and too long to its pet dogmas, till its future came to depend on upholding the creed. Such was the vested interest of the church in upholding its doctrinaire declarations as sacrosanct that those who believed the world to be round and not flat were killed and those who said our globe circled a steady sun and not vice-versa were seen fit to be blinded. Such has been your understanding and your tolerance.

"I am showing you now, Reverend Pastor, the centrality of consciousness in creation. A vedic declaration says *'Prajñānam*

Brahma', meaning 'Total Consciousness is God.' How can words divide the Truth? Different societies in the world, with their different languages, have come up with their own words for God. Words are only sound-symbols for our communication.

"What is all-important is consciousness. And the voice of consciousness reverberates as 'I am'. Self-recognition of existence starts with its own I-am-ness, and then 'you', 'they', and all other objects are recognized. Your Gospel distilled the whole truth of the God-concept into one word 'Jehovah' – 'I am that I am.' How precise, how beautiful! God, asked to reveal himself to the human mind through a description of Himself, could only say "I am the I-am-ness." Beyond that, words fail and silence prevails. It is the silence that speaks to silence.

"I-am-ness is God. But in our personalized human experience, 'I am' gets the false connotation that 'I' am this person, this egocentric personality. So the correction of the primordial error lies in the transcendence from limitation. Total Consciousness is unlimited and unqualified. To that Absolute Existence is given the name GOD. See it this way: if that perfection were to speak of itself, what other words can announce its existence, other than 'I AM the Creator' or 'I AM Perfection'? 'I AM' is inevitable, and correct. That is as it should be.

"Now see, in personal terms of you and me, what appears to have transpired. The ego-person, the individualized entity has emerged. He too is of the nature of consciousness and therein he is not different from God-nature essentially.

"But he is limited as an individual, one of many, and identified with his body and its history. He says: I AM this person, this is my family, these are my possessions. 'I AM' is the substratum always, but with reference to God (or god-idea), it is total, eternal, unchanging, whereas with reference to man, it is limited, conditioned and temporal.

"This is and has always been the Truth, but we are yet to see it. All these sages who, having seen it, are trying to show it to us through scripture or speech are the sons of God. And they are telling us that all the rest of us are equally sons of God once we know the truth of ourselves. That is the call to 'know thyself'. We do not get elevated to sit on the right side of God in paradise forever more; it is a merger, we become one with God. The son of God is God. Language is relative, what it indicates is Absolute.

"But you have lost the sense of what Christ spoke and what he transcended. You believe that Christ was the only son of God and all other humans were sinners. At your behest, they will be saved. Your call is 'All ye sinners, come here and be saved', whereas the call of the Hindu sages is 'All ye children of immortal bliss, know thy own true nature'. Are those who regard humanity as 'all ye sinners' going to convert and lead to the kingdom of God those who have the vision to address humanity as 'children of immortal bliss'?

"Now can you appreciate, Pastor, what 'conversion' should rightly mean? It has a deep import, but you know nothing of it. It means: Man should convert himself to God. The humanized I-ness must be divinized once again by realizing its own potential. This is called enlightenment, self-realization, transcendence. This, sir, is conversion.

"And you want to sprinkle water three times on a forehead, and change the person's name, and thereby you will change the person's faith and ensure one's happiness in life and after-life! He whom you teach to betray his faith in his personal god will be ready to betray all values in life later. You are selling betrayal, not faith.

"You know our child is sick. You know we are financially strained. You know we have been Hindus for generations. And you see your opportunity here. All you have is a petty love for yourself, as this prized conquest will enhance your prestige and advance your career and add strength by multiplier effect to your church. Are you in the business of saving or of enslaving souls?

"Wherefore does the church spend 150 billion dollars globally in one year? Why does it have four million full-time workers and 2000 radio and T.V. stations? Why does it keep on buying up and controlling the media? Why is it the policy of the church to target schools and hospitals? Is it not because the vulnerable in the form of young minds and sick bodies can thus be exploited for your conversions? Are you merchants of benevolence or merchants of violence who hold a morsel to the mouth while holding a dagger to the soul?

"Let it be declared that Christianity has gone, only churchianity remains. You are desperate to reinforce your failing grip in your countries of origin by conquering new territory in Asia, Africa and South America with money power and technological strengths.

"Want a laugh, Pastor? Listen to what the great Desmond Tutu said in South Africa years back: 'When missionaries came, we had the land and they had the bible. We closed our eyes to pray; when we opened them, we found that they had the land and we had the bible!' And now we are in the same boat – *Bhārata*, my motherland, should I laugh or weep?

"As in a dream, the mind of the dreamer is the only creative agent and energy, and a whole world of seeming reality assumes existence for the dreamer, so is cosmic creation the manifestation of the Supreme Consciousness which is God.

"The whole of this multitudinous creation is God, only God, and nothing but God. Hills and rivers, plants, birds, fish, snakes and other animals are all as exclusively the stuff of God as we humans are. So what is pagan, heathen, or animist about the Hindu who rightly sees God in all created things and offers them homage that is due to God? It is you who lack the vision and the understanding.

"Take back with you, Pastor, the words of one of the greatest sages, Ramana Maharṣhi, our contemporary. He has said: 'Amongst the many thousands of names for God, who abides in the heart devoid of thought, no other name suits Him so truly, aptly, and beautifully as the name "I" or "I am". Of all the known names of God, the name of God as the unbroken "I-I-I" continuum, no other, will resound triumphantly when the ego is destroyed.' Convert yourself, Pastor, into a seeker of truth."

Silence and stillness followed. Then all stood up. The Pastor tried to put on a brave face. Seeming to say an unperturbed farewell to all, he mumbled something, and looking Geeta squarely in the eye, he added, "If ever needed, my offer still stands. It is not withdrawn." With that, he left.

Divya called from her room. "Thatha, has the visitor left?"

"Have you been awake, Divya, or did we wake you up?"

"Partly awake, Thatha, and partly drowsy. Thatha, you were speaking for a long, long while."

"I had a short, short message to convey!"

"I could hear it, in bits and pieces, whenever I was awake. What I heard, Thatha, was a better tranquilizer than anything the doctor gave!"

"You sleep now."

"I will. I can."

※

28

Geeta was sobbing bitterly, her grief nearly driving her hysterical. She came up and touched her father-in-law's feet as if to say she was speaking with all reverence and she said through her tears, "Father, forgive me if I trespass, but I cannot understand what is happening. I think you turned down the pastor's offer. Why? How will we get twenty lakhs now? God, I may lose my Divya. I cannot think of living without her. What was the unacceptable block in the offer? Even now it is open."

"Dear daughter," said Raman, "do we not understand your feelings when our own feelings are the same? But there are some things in our lives that are not negotiable and the faith of the soul is foremost amongst them. Govinda has left to talk to his chairman. On the pledge of this house, he may raise much of the money now needed, but please understand that the outcome cannot change the absolute values of life. Our faith cannot go on one track if we have our own money and on another track if we do not.

Geeta, there is only one God and He does not respond to a name, He responds to the faith. You have been praying to God, continue the prayers, they are being heard, and whatever is right and righteous in terms of cosmic causality will befall us. We cannot demand whatever we desire; we must be able to see the rightness in what He gives. There is no beginning called 'birth', so there can be no ending called 'death'. In the reign of Time, we are all immortal through recurrent mortality. But in our union with God, we transcend to a timeless truth of eternal life. Let that blessing come to us. Meanwhile, we will do what we can and leave the rest to God."

Govinda called, losing no time to convey the good news, and informed Geeta that his company had sanctioned a loan of twenty lakhs, rightly valuing his residential property at over thirty lakhs at the prevailing rates for real estate in the area. He was going to meet Dr. Shankar to request rushing the import of the required life-saving materials from abroad. The happy tidings gave some respite to Geeta.

Divya was feeling better the next morning and a faint smile had returned to her face. She came and sat with her Thatha in the front verandah, where a mild sun warmed them. "Thatha," she asked, "from all that I have heard in bits and pieces, I understand that my condition is serious. I also believe that treatment for me costs much more than we can afford. I am not afraid or worried for myself, Thatha, but I am sad to see Mummy crying. I am also troubled thinking of my brother Niranjan. We need money for his professional education, and I am coming in the way."

Ramana Thatha interrupted her. He said, "Divya, it is better you leave these matters to the elders. Do not think about them. Just wish that you should get well and strong soon. We can manage the funds."

"I know, Thatha, I heard that Daddy's company will help us. But there is something else I want to know. It can happen to someone else if not to me, that is why I want to know the answer. Thatha, if there is not enough money to carry out the complete treatment for a case of leukaemia, would you say that the patient died of the disease, or of poverty?"

Raman took a while to digest the implication of the precocious question, and then spoke in a pensive and measured tone. "Dear child," he said, "I have told you this before and I will repeat it now: death was never born and life never died. He who imagines he was born will one day imagine that he died, both being figments of thought-waves in consciousness. Such a human will naturally experience rebirth and exist as another person. It is in that cycle of birth, death and rebirth that you and I are now the persons that we take ourselves to be. This is a relative reality, and every aspect of this experience is conditioned by duality. Your question arises from such paired and opposed concepts, health and sickness, riches and poverty, life and death. The answers can only reflect mental dispositions and cannot claim to be facts.

"Your question may be answered either way: that an incurable cancer killed the patient, or that lack of money made the cure inaccessible. How do we know that the patient would have survived if money had been available? How do we know that no amount of money could have brought him back to life? It is all speculation. What is not speculation is the seeming fact that every one dies. And I am telling you, Divya, that no one dies, that death is a myth because life itself was an illusion.

Why then should we be concerned with the causes of death? The only cause for all death is when the causal relationship between the mind and its environment has exhausted its connectivity. Then the mind goes its way and the body goes to the grave. There can be no loss or gain to the mind until it frees itself from this false circle. From relative reality of apparent truth, let our minds be centred in Absolute Reality, in the Truth. This human body is not you; you are pure Consciousness. Let not your mind waver any more. Live this knowledge, Divya, and you will feel your unity with God."

"Thatha, it is always so helpful to talk to you. You have fully answered my question by fully dismissing it! You have also moved me to reach the point where there can be no questions any more. I only wish Mummy could see it that way. Thatha, how do people live their lives without the strength of this knowledge?"

"That is the great mystery and the great tragedy: human beings go on enduring so much sorrow and suffering, never learning, and still hoping that abiding happiness will come to them on the same path.

"You go in now, Divya, and chat with Mummy. Then rest. You are not cured yet, and the doctor may call you for chemotherapy to prepare you for the stem-cell transplant. There are hard days ahead, my gentle child, and your body will have to endure a lot of pain. I would rather that you know it, and accept it, than that we draw a veil over the situation. Stand apart from your body, making it an object of your detached perception. And even go farther; stand detached from all of us. Stand centred in your own self. Try, Divya, and you can succeed. All that I have told you is sanctioned by our scriptures. *Avadhūta Gītā*, a sublime spiritual text, declares:

Vedāhnalokāhnasurāhnayajñāh

(There are no vedas, no worlds, no gods, no sacrifices.)

"The *śloka* goes on to say that there is only the highest Truth, the homogeneous Brahman. So, you see, there is nothing else to understand or to do, one must get established in the I-ness of oneself, that is all. Turn the mind inward, Divya, go into your self, by yourself. In the Absolute, silence is the only speech." Divya held her Thatha's hand tightly and stood silent. Then she let go of the hand and went in.

Later in the day, when Govinda returned home and Niranjan too was back, they all sat together. Govinda told them that he had spoken to Dr. Shankar about the fifteen lakh rupees that would be paid as advance to the hospital. On that assurance, the import of cord blood had been confirmed, and the material was expected to reach the hospital within seven days.

Niranjan's results had been announced, and unfortunately, he had missed the cut-off point for free admission to most engineering courses by two marks. His had been a creditable performance in troubled times, but luck had not favoured him. "Do not worry, Niranjan," his father told him. "You can come into our company as an apprentice on a stipend. I will be there to guide and supervise your work. You start hands-on as a grease monkey and work your way up. You will get to know the machines, and what's more, you will imbibe the dignity of labour. You will progress through maintenance to operations.

"At the end of one year, the practical training would have raised you to a level where your grasp of the practical side of engineering will be greatly enhanced. We will try to get you into an engineering course at that time. But right now, Divya has to be the priority."

"I understand, Daddy. I want Divya back home and healthy," Niranjan said.

Raman nodded approvingly.

❦

29

Two days later, Dr. Shankar called them to his office and said Divya should be admitted into the hospital. She would need to be prepared for the transplantation by a conditioning treatment. "High doses of drugs are administered to completely destroy the existing diseased bone marrow and thereby help the patient to receive the new stem cells. Numerous individual injections and regular doses of drugs will be required over several weeks, for which a tube known as a central line will again be inserted. After initial chemotherapy, the patient will feel a little better. The cord blood will be given then through the central line into a vein, through a drip, like a blood transfusion. The stem cells will find their way through the bloodstream to the bones, where they will hopefully start to grow and develop into mature blood cells.

"It may take two weeks for signs to appear that the new bone marrow is growing. Divya will remain alone in a single room for protection against the risk of infection. Two to three weeks after the transplantation, the blood count is at its lowest and the risks then are at a maximum. After six to eight weeks, Divya will be able to leave the hospital. When the marrow is recovering, there is a risk of potentially life-threatening infections and bleeding. Being properly informed will make it easier for her and the family, and therefore I am giving you the full details," Dr. Shankar said.

Geeta asked, barely holding back her tears, "Doctor, you can save my child? Will she become all right?"

He replied gently, "Mother, you are a religious person. The divine saint Ramakrishna Paramahansa said that God smiles to Himself at two conceits of the human mind: one, when two brothers, dividing their property between themselves, draw a line across their land and announce, this side of the line is my land and that side is yours! God sees in it the vanity of a bubble laying claim to eternity. God smiles again when a doctor says that he will save the life of a patient. The doctor may imagine he is the great performer, but, in truth, it is the cosmic will that decides all events, life and death included. I will do my utmost. What more can I promise you?"

Govinda took Geeta's hand. They thanked the doctor before leaving. Divya would get admitted the next day.

At home, Divya was unperturbed. She laughed and said, "The hospital has become my second house!" She spent the interval in visiting her friends in the neighbourhood, remaining calmer than all of them.

When it was time to leave for the hospital, she picked up her favourite doll, held it to her cheek for a moment, then said: "No, sweetie. They won't allow you into the hospital. You may catch an infection. So you sit here and wait for me." Divya started to leave, then halted. She turned round and walked up to the doll. "I'll tell you what we'll do. I will place you on the windowsill facing the main gate. That way, when I return, you'll be the first one to see me and greet me." So saying, she moved the doll to the windowsill, patted it, and left.

It was arranged that Divya would stay for two days in a double-occupancy ward before being moved into isolation. It happened that Kumar, a boy of about her age, also afflicted by leukaemia, with complications of the kidneys and the liver, was the other occupant of the ward. He had come to the hospital a year and a half back and had been in and out since then. He had found a matching donor in his brother, and had had a bone marrow transplant operation done. There had been hopes of recovery, but he had suddenly deteriorated to a critical level, and the doctors were discussing shifting him to an associated super-speciality division.

Divya and Kumar had met earlier as two patients with the same medical problem, and spoken to each other occasionally. One day, Kumar had said, "I am afraid I may die, Divya."

She had replied, "Everyone has to die one day, Kumar. My grandpa has taught me this: Death is certain, the hour of death is uncertain."

"I am too young to die, Divya."

"The same goes for me too, Kumar. Death is a physical reality, fear is a mental perception. Why court sorrow for something that may not happen? Let us live day by day and maybe we will live year after year. Cheer up, Kumar. What do you want to do when you grow up?" Thus the little professor had tried to tell Kumar a little of the deeper truths she had heard and understood from Thatha, but she also knew that to say more would be beyond Kumar's reach now. An inner call was reminding her of the ultimate Reality, the transcendence beyond body and pain, beyond life and death, beyond time and space and all duality – that was the Truth of God and His creation, wherein, amazingly, the Creator and the creature were one!

Kumar stirred in his bed, opened drowsy eyes and said, "Is

that you, Divya? How are you? You have come back?" and then, breathlessly, "Mummy, it is too much, the pain is too much, I can't bear it. Mummy, call them, do something." His mother could only stand by his side, for this was a constantly repeated occurrence, and the main recourse seemed to be sedation. In a while, the sedation began to take effect and Kumar lay still.

His mother came to Divya's bedside. Geeta put an arm round her – they were two mothers sharing a common fate. Their understanding was wordlessly complete, their hearts beat in unison, and their emotions resonated to the same shrill pitch. "Kumar's bone marrow transplant has failed," said his mother. "There is no hope left. We are standing by. The doctors are acting on what they think is the last chance." She moved and spoke like a robot. When life moves beyond the known bounds of endurance, probably we are given the energy to endure the excess more easily. "We will be shifted in two hours," she said, and moved back to her son. Her son of sixteen years, and what would he be like sixteen hours later?

Divya was made to get into her bed, and the nurses and the medicos moved in and out, checking weight, temperature and blood pressure, taking blood samples, giving a series of injections. A couple of hours passed, and a stretcher was brought to take Kumar to the ambulance. The nurses lifted him ever so carefully, yet he screamed in pain. "It is killing me," he wailed. "Every bone is aching unbearably." Then he looked out with haunted eyes and cried, "I don't want to die. Mummy. I want to live, I want to live." The words faded as he receded. An eerie silence fell for a while. Then the same routine bustle was resumed.

Family members could visit Divya now, but later there would be restrictions. Divya knew that she would not have many more opportunities to converse with her Thatha. So when he came in to be with her early that evening, she grasped the chance to ask him one more question. "Thatha," she asked, "why is it necessary for so much pain to attend a fatal sickness? When one is dying, why should one be made to endure so much pain? Nature could have ordained that a person just dies painlessly. What purpose does this pain serve, Thatha?"

Thatha said, "Recently I was reading *Memoirs of a Vagrant Soul* by Mikhail Naimy, a Persian author of Sufi persuasions. In it, the same question is raised and an answer is attempted. I remember it vividly. When asked why sometimes a dying person should suffer pain, the answer vouchsafed by the author is: How do you know that a dying person is not on a pilgrimage and that his pains this side of the grave are not his food for a journey the other side of the grave? If it were otherwise, your life and all life would be a travesty – a thing devoid of all meaning. For, what could be the meaning of a life entirely effaced by Death?

"You can see, Divya, that the answer is addressed to one who assumes that death is a zero-point, an annihilation, an end in a void. This concept is vigorously corrected by the author. It is said that the pain is a final settlement of accounts for the accrued causes he created for himself in his life, a debt he repays at the time of his death, as he should. Relieved of the debt and freed of the pain when he is freed from the physical bondage, the subtle body, which exists beyond the gross body's grave, has this freedom for its food and strength. Were it not true that the psyche of the person continues its mental existence through a long pilgrimage of rebirths, there would be a travesty of reason and logic in lives begun without cause and ended without effect.

"This, Divya, would be all that we could have finally told Kumar as he parted from us with pain and fear. He cannot now understand a truth that goes beyond that. He can only be helped to vanquish his pain through the knowledge of the spirit's survival beyond death. But, with you, it is different. You have been a spiritual seeker instinctively, and therefore insights which elude many intelligent persons in a lifetime have been opened for you at a tender age.

"The goal of life lies in the separative ego recognizing its oneness with the Total Consciousness. Mind is not the product of matter. The brain is a part of the physical body. Like muscle, blood, bone or heart, it is made of matter imbibed through food, and structured with chemical differences. The brain is also matter, therefore, and matter is inert, insentient. But to have consciousness is to be alive and sentient. Can 'dead' matter produce 'life'? It is a contradiction in terms. The brain cannot 'produce' consciousness. It is the instrument through which the energy of consciousness manifests as perception and sensation, and leads to action.

"For example, you know that electricity is a kind of energy. It is not 'produced' by the bulb or the fan. Those are matched equipment through which electricity manifests as visible light or motion. Matter cannot 'produce' energy. The brain acts mechanically when touched by the power of consciousness, and nerves are the 'wiring' to transport the energy inside the body.

"Divya, you are not the body – that is the equipment through which consciousness expresses as memory. Having transcended the fragmented and limited ego-sense, you are united with pure Total Consciousness. How can death be a concern for one like you? Know this also clearly, Divya – enlightenment of the spirit is not linked to bodily existence or death. *Jivanmukti* is liberation while in the physical frame.

"While talking to you about the human's ascendance to his potential of divinity, I often tell you about the life and teachings of Bhagavan Ramana Maharishi because he was the palpable and living proof of this astounding truth. He was contemporaneous for people of my generation. He was born near Madurai in 1880. At the age of sixteen, enlightenment happened to him and in him. He was drawn to the spiritual eminence of Arunachala Hill in Thiruvannamalai and lived there, fulfilled and ecstatic, till 1950. That makes him to us more real, more credible, and more visible than the sages and *ṛshis* and divinities of ancient lore. In time and space, he was so close to us.

We have inherited him through his written and spoken words, and the numerous recountals of his life. This great sage used to live and move with ordinary people like us, while, in reality, he was in the state of *mukti* or liberation, Absolute beyond the taint of relativity. He too, Divya, was inflicted by an extremely painful form of cancer, or rather, his body was subjected to it, not he – in his experience, he was not the body. The pain racked that body, yet the pain was not his. Nor could our idea of death apply to him. One day, near the end of that body's tenure, a close devotee of Bhagavan was shedding copious tears. Bhagavan kindly asked, 'Ramachandra Iyer, why these tears?' He replied, sobbing, 'I am afraid Bhagavan may leave us.' Bhagavan said, 'What talk is this! Where will Bhagavan go? Where *can* he go?' Imbibe the true meaning of those words, Divya. Nothing need be said beyond that. I have told you everything."

The evening fell. Divya's eyes were aglow with the light of surpassing knowledge. Such knowledge is itself compassion, therefore tentative tears trembled in her eyes, reflecting a grief not her own. It was her unrelieved grief for a faltering society that bears its burden of relentless suffering without realizing that the purpose of human life is not to bear the yoke of submission to an illusory subjugation, but to rediscover the bliss of self-sufficiency and freedom. "Who am I?" is the right question; "I am this embodied person" is the wrong answer. Without ever enquiring into this vital and all-consuming question, humanity stumbles from cradle to grave, dragging the chain of time.

Divya was grateful to God that she had been given Ramana Thatha who always wanted her mind to be centred in the Truth of the Creator who was one's own Self. This ultimate Reality is veiled by the concept of being the body, ruled by time and doomed to die. She was blessed to have the right knowledge now.

Slowly, her eyelids closed and she slept in peace.

❦

30

Another day. It was evening and the shadow play of rustling leaves, lightly traced upon the wall, indicated the descending sun. Divya, regardless of her bodily state, was brimming with life, her mind totally alert, her senses totally awake. She had a question that seemed to be all-consuming and she could not resolve it. There was an urgency to ask her Raman Thatha about it and fortunately there was the opportunity too.

Divya was the only patient in the ward, Kumar having been shifted – to which space? to what destiny? – and she could talk with Ramana Thatha without distraction. Tomorrow, she would be moved into isolation.

"Thatha."

"Yes, Divya."

"Thatha, I know what I know, and you know what it is because it is you who taught me this knowledge. Life and death are concepts that acquire reality in relation to the body of the person referred to. We say a person was born and later say the person died. Life manifests in the body at birth and withdraws at death. The withdrawal is what is called death. It may be the right word with reference to the body, but it is irrelevant with reference to the psyche. The energizing consciousness that we call life remains intact and continues to function on its pattern of causality, which is cause-effect continuity. That is cosmic determinism. Am I right so far, Thatha?"

"You are right so far, child."

"Just now, we would say the sun is 'setting' upon our land. But in reality, the sun is not moving. Our land, because of the earth's rotation, is moving out of the sun's light, which remains constant, and therefore our stretch of land becomes dark. Day and night alternate only for he who stands upon the earth. If he could stand upon the sun, he would see nothing but light eternally and the duality of day and night would be meaningless. The sun never rises, never sets.

"You have told me I am Consciousness. I am that Power, that Person, that *Purusha* which shines as the Light of life. That is the Truth, the Reality, of Divya, and Divya must find the true centre. That is what I wish for myself, and that is what you wish for me too. Am I right, Thatha?"

"You are right, my child."

"I have also learnt from you, Thatha, that the ego of the individual, caught in the ignorance of limitation through body-identification, cannot escape the compulsive sense of being an independent centre of willing, sensing, and acting. Thus, it seems to devolve upon us to choose our course of action in the circumstances in which we find ourselves in the progression of time.

"Therefore, my father and mother feel called upon, by the very fact of parenthood, to try to save my life from the threat of cancer. They have dealt with it meticulously and have been implementing the best possible treatment to control and cure the malady. I reckon about thirty lakh rupees have already been spent, which means our resources and reserves are already exhausted.

"And yet, there seems to be a long way to go before it would be possible to affirm whether I will be cured or not. The demand may be for another thirty lakhs, without any guarantee of survival. By then, the family will be too deeply into debt, Niranjan's hopes will be in tatters, careers will be shredded, and Thatha, in the evening of your life, you will be a witness to these shattered dreams and troubles.

"So, the question arises in me, Thatha – how can it not? – why don't we remain silent spectators henceforth of what destiny has in store for me, without spending on further treatment? We cannot foretell the future. A favourable result too, if it should come, will come at a cost that destroys no less than what it saves. Thatha, why should I not accept death without resistance, if it already has one foot in my doorway?

"I am not inviting death; I know death gives no gifts. I do not seek to deny whatever pain may be due. I am only saying: let nature run its course without our resorting to desperate remedies. In a storm, would one anchor a ship with a load that by itself could sink the vessel? Thatha, if the time has come, let Divya die."

Silence. There were only the sounds within Raman's mind of his words of reply, before they could be spoken. The mellow sun was poised above the horizon, tarrying there to caress Divya's cheeks a moment longer. Ramana Thatha gazed into the eyes that were looking at him, peaceful, alert, questing for the highest knowledge but content to wait.

Thatha considered his answer thoughtfully. The undertones of Divya's query were deep and subtle. If the higher direction of mental evolution consists of surrender to cosmic sequencing, with the ego-person remaining an unresisting witness to all events, come what may, where is the need for personal effort to stem or to turn the tide of destiny?

He decided that he would answer her without compromise if he had to, but there was another immediate aspect that would make more practical sense to her. In terms of the Absolute, Divya was right. But, at the moment, there was still the need for decisions and actions to be evaluated at the relative level of egocentric personality.

Therefore, he said: "Divya, your conclusions are not justified. But, that apart, the decisions have been taken, the commitments have been made, money has already been paid to the hospital for cord blood transplant. We have to go ahead with the treatment. There is no scope left to think of expenditure."

"I am aware of that, too, Thatha," said Divya. "But we can still try. If you permit, I will speak to Dr. Shankar myself. I will request him to use the imported cord blood for another patient and refund our money to us. They have so many patients, and I am sure it will match someone else. The product can be stored for a long time. We can give it a try. Please, Thatha."

"Divya, the doctor cannot suspend your treatment at this stage. It is professionally unethical; I think it is illegal too. It may amount to homicide. The concept of 'mercy killing' is rejected in our system."

"Excuse me, Thatha, but that is not the case with me. The treatment has not started. I am not on life-support. I can express my wish, even my decision. I mean, your decision." She smiles. "Thatha…?"

"Divya, let us now probe deeply the perplexed question of Karma and free will. Thereafter, you be the judge and pronounce the verdict. We have a rational concept of Karma as a continuity of cause-effect sequences, with inescapable and infallible determinism, as certain causes can only produce given effects. Yet, since the mind always thinks of opposites, and functions in comparison between opposed dualities, it cannot abandon the concept of freedom of its own will.

"Whence comes this notion of liberty? It persists because there is no existence of an ego that is a separate reality, severed from Total Consciousness. It is derived from the cosmic manifestation of Consciousness and retains the original truth of itself intact, with connotations of Will, Existence, Energy and Bliss. Yet, being the product of an assumed Ignorance in the Totality, it lives completely in an arbitrary illusion of its mentality.

"There is no free choice at the point of the ego-centre, but only the Will and the Choice that are the workings of a past impulsion from the movement of Total Conscious Energy which includes the ego's temporality, the present environment, the web of interactions receding into the obscure past – why, the eternity of time, the infinity of space, and the limitless play of Total Mind.

"We do not act, we are made to act. Our phantom will is an instrument of a transcendental Will and Intelligence that is aware of itself and its own play amidst its reflections, but we have located ourselves behind the veil of ignorance called *Avidyā*, and our falsified knowledge of relativity only testifies to our ignorance of the Absolute.

"See the truth of that, Divya, and you will see that however finite our sense of personal life and mind and body, we are participating in the workings of Infinity. Whether you express your preference to live or die, it has its origin in the vaster circle of your entire life, relationships and environment.

"By the same token then, I, your parents, the doctor, and all the rest who have been drawn into this circle of decision and action, have each his or her personal will, operating under the same impulse of Totality, but believing mistakenly that it is an option. What will you tell them? Will you say you are right and they are wrong?

"The truth is, Divya, that there is no determinable right or wrong in this or in any assessment of relativity. There is no error in the workings of the Divine Law based on oneness. What should transpire in the rigid rightness of causal justification is the justice meted out to mortals. If you say let there be no intervention with Nature, such refusal of action too is an act of intervention with Nature.

"You may live and fulfil yourself. Or you may die fulfilled. Or you may die without completing the journey, and bear the consequences. Who knows? Who can tell? We can have hopes, but no certitude. Therefore, Divya, we will do what our discrimination decrees and our abilities aspire for.

"Finally, and transcending all other perceptions, let this alone engage your attention: By now, through the power of true knowledge, Divya-the-person has ceased to be. To yourself, you are Divya no more, you are pure Consciousness. There is no Divya on whom Karma can impact anymore. There are no parents, no Thatha, no doctor. There is no body, no cancer, no death.

"That must be the living truth for you, blessed child, now cradled in the arms of God. You are already beyond the progressions of life or the fatality of death. Those that are still subject to karmic ignorance will have to live the fantasies of their minds, and they will. They do not exist to Divya, though Divya exists to them.

"Think no more, blessed soul that has been reunited to your source. Let it rest there, precious child. Let events run their course. The financial scene is not too grim. Though it is a burden that strains the sinews, it can and will be borne. I need not offer you consolation by saying 'All will be well'. The truth is that 'All that happens is always well'. That is the Lord's law."

Divya held Thatha's hand. Then she threw her arms round his neck, saying softly, "*Shambho ta va aaradhanam.*"

31

D estiny hangs in the balance. Divya is in the isolation
ward under thoroughly sanitized conditions. Only her
mother is allowed to be with her at monitored intervals,
subject to precautions.

Divya's diseased bone marrow is aspirated to cleanse the system,
preparatory to the induction of new stem cells through cord blood
transplant. One last cycle of treatment with chemotherapeutic
drugs is administered. She is subjected to cranial radiotherapy
to forestall the spread of cancerous cells into the nervous system.
When chemotherapy is finished, she starts to feel a little better.
After that, it is time for the transplant.

The cord blood is given to her through the central line, into a
vein; the stem cells it contains will find their way into the bones,
where they will start to grow and mature into blood cells. In two
weeks, the new blood cells will be released into the bloodstream.
The recovery will have started.

The days pass by slowly, too slowly, while hope is suspended
on gossamer threads. Govinda the person goes daily to the factory;
Govinda the father lingers in the hospital corridors. Niranjan the
brother goes to his new workplace for training, his hands busy

in labour but his mind benumbed. Raman stays partly at home and partly outside the glass doors of Divya's room, his mind unfathomable to others.

And Geeta, what can be said of Geeta: a mother's heart in dread and despair, hot irons of fear piercing her constantly, her tears flowing uncontrollably. She goes to numerous temples, crying "All ye gods, won't someone listen to me and save my Divya?" She requests the priests to perform special poojas at her house, conduct *homams* and *yajñas*, whatever will invoke protection. The sacred smoke floats through the rooms, the chiming of bells fills the air, the chants reverberate, the holy fire rises, fed by ghee. The lamps burn while the oil lasts, then flicker and fade away.

Kumar's life could not be saved. Three days after he was shifted, he died. Geeta heard the news and shivered and wept for Kumar and for herself. She kept it to herself, not wanting Divya to know it. But maybe Divya overheard the nurses or doctors talking about it, or maybe she sensed it from something her mother said or did; somehow Divya guessed or came to know what had happened. "Kumar is dead, Mummy, and he so longed to live. What actually happens has the weight of reality behind it, what we wish to the contrary is illusion."

Geeta stares ahead blankly, unable to decipher what Divya may be implying by such talk – is she saying she will live or that she too will die? Kumar, you had no right to die, not after you had a transplant. You see, we have done a transplant on Divya, and she cannot die any more. Otherwise, what is the sense of all this trouble, this cost, this pain, this desperate hope? Kumar, you should not have died. You will see, Divya will live on. Oh, what am I saying? You will not be there to see her. Thus goes Geeta's rant within her disturbed mind.

Time is marching on leaden feet, but there is no improvement in Divya's condition. It is two weeks since the transplant and there is no improvement in the blood count. Her bones have lost their natural character, and there is acute pain in all of them. Her whole body hurts unbearably. Her mother lays loving hands on her two arms, only to bring out a sudden scream from Divya – "Don't touch me!" – a rude, desperate cry because even a gentle touch crushes her like a hammer blow. The others cannot comprehend it, but her pain is real. Divya relents, "Sorry, Mummy. Please do not hold me. It hurts so much, I can't bear the pain, Mummy." Then she groans and moans.

Dr. Shankar comes. He has the latest blood report in his hand. You can see he is a broken man. He knows where human skills have reached their limits. Infection will not hurt Divya any more, for she is beyond that. Divya is dying. Govinda is asked to come in. There is no need for words, yet they must be spoken. Dr. Shankar has tears in his eyes. He looks at Govinda and Geeta. "I am sorry. We tried our best, but we are unable to save her. The transplant has failed. She has only a few hours left. She has great pain; we will tranquilize her, it may give some relief." Divya opens her eyes, groans, and closes her eyes.

The doctor arranges for her to be moved, cradled in soft sheets, to a larger ward adjacent to the isolation ward. Nothing matters any more. Here the family can gather round her. Only an hour or two are left. The grandfather is there too. The brother comes. Uncles, aunts, cousins… without crowding the place, they come, they see, they stifle their sobs, and they slowly step out. Raman stays by her side, the grandfather watching the granddaughter. Watching her die? But there is no death, that is the distilled wisdom, he tells himself. Wisdom, true. But here, before you, is the experience. There must be some reconciliation. There is. And there is not.

Divya opens her eyes. A new surge of life shines in them like a light. The bright eyes look steadily at father, mother and brother, and hold their eyes captive in turns. A smile lingers on her lips, though the face winces again and again with pain. They all mutter some words, unable to bear the silence. Then Divya turns her eyes upon her Thatha. The eyes are glowing with an inward rapture that communicates through the avalanche of pain descending on her. "Thatha."

"Yes, Divya."

"Thatha, they think I am going. But my travels are over. I am at peace, Thatha, because of what you have taught me. Tell them I am at peace, Thatha, and let them be at peace. Farewell, dear Thatha, fare thee well." And she closes her eyes.

Her breathing becomes visibly laboured. Two nurses come and hurriedly check her pulse and blood pressure. One of them rushes out and returns with Dr. Shankar. He lifts her eyelids and looks. He holds her limp wrist. The face of Death is all too familiar to him, for Death is frequently stalking or striking in a cancer hospital. The doctor recognizes it instantly. He gently pulls the white sheet over Divya's face.

He instructs the staff to prepare the body to be taken home (Home? Raman wonders). The doctor takes Govinda aside and tells him, "The rules are that all bills are fully paid and then the body is removed. But the formalities will take time, so I will issue special instructions in this case. You please arrange to pay the bills after three or four days. You may take the body now. Ambulance will be ready." He stops, hesitates, then speaks, "Please allow me… I will forego my personal fees for the transplant. Just to show my… my…" He turns round and walks away.

It is a beautiful day. A mild sun is watching the earth. Clusters of clouds are spread across the sky. A cool breeze blows. Divya's body is gently slid into the ambulance. Geeta steps in, saying, "My baby may call me." No one prevents her.

As they pass along the road, a brief, light shower of rain falls, as if the heavens want to sprinkle blessings upon Divya. The sun continues to shine, and the scattered raindrops continue to fall. And looking up at the sky, one suddenly sees a rainbow spanning the open spaces, with lovely tints of varied hues, all born of the sun's whiteness, to mingle again and merge into the source. Raman sees it and gently feels the confirmation that Divya knows what should be known.

At home, the priests are performing a pooja. The vedic chants go on, linking creation to cosmic energies, the power of the *mantra* and the supplication of the soul blended to command and to plead simultaneously. As Divya's body is slowly carried to the verandah, the doll upon the windowsill stares mutely and the strains of the chant are heard; the chaste Sanskrit *ślokas* of *yakshmanivaraṇa* from *Ātharvaṇa Vedā* are being recited by the priests who are unaware of Divya's demise (Does that matter?):

Headache, head pain, earache, inflammations,
All that now afflicts the head,
Expel we by our prayer.
The pains that suck the marrow out
And cleave and rend the bones asunder,
Let them go forth at the orifice,
Without ill effect, harmless.
The wasting diseases that numb the limbs,
Racking the frame with colic pains,
The poison of every wasting disease
From you I exorcise.

❦

www.ingramcontent.com/pod-product-compliance
Lightning Source LLC
Chambersburg PA
CBHW062220080426
42734CB00010B/1970